INNOVATIONS IN THE CARE OF THE ELDERLY

INNOVATIONS IN THE CARE OF THE ELDERLY

EDITED BY
BERNARD ISAACS
AND HELEN EVERS

CROOM HELM
London • Sydney • Dover, New Hampshire

© 1984 Bernard Isaacs and Helen Evers
Croom Helm Ltd, Provident House, Burrell Row,
Beckenham, Kent BR3 1AT
Croom Helm Australia Pty Ltd, First Floor, 139 King Street,
Sydney, NSW 2001, Australia

British Library Cataloguing in Publication Data

Innovations in the care of the elderly.
　　1. Aged—Services for—England—
　　Birmingham (West Midlands)
　　I. Isaacs, Bernard　II. Evers, Helen
　　362.6'09424'96　　HV1481.G55B5

　　ISBN 0-7099-1310-9
　　ISBN 0-7099-1317-6 Pbk

Croom Helm, 51 Washington Street, Dover,
New Hampshire 03820, USA

Library of Congress Catalog Card Number: 84-45554
Cataloging in Publication Data applied for.

Printed and bound in Great Britain
by Billing & Sons Limited, Worcester.

CONTENTS

Contents

TABLES AND FIGURES

Tables

Figures

ACKNOWLEDGEMENTS

We would like to thank Brenda Waller for her patience and enthusiasm in typing various drafts as well as the final manuscript.

INTRODUCTION

Bernard Isaacs

This book describes some of the innovations in the care of the elderly which took place in and around Birmingham in the late 1970s and early 1980s. The book focuses on one care group and one place; but despite this, or perhaps because of this, it claims to have more than local or specialist interest. It describes the fine detail of innovation, and the interaction of one change on another. It is about innovation and how this is perceived; and about change and how this is achieved. It should be helpful to would-be innovators in other fields and in other locations.

There were several reasons why this flurry of innovation in the care of the elderly took place in the West Midlands in the late 1970s. These included: the social pressure of a growing number of old people in need; the political desirability of being seen to be doing something about it; the economic need to make more effective use of limited resources; the opportunities provided by specially designated funds; and two major attitudinal shifts - from institutional to community care, and from service-orientated to client-orientated provision. Against this background active people with good ideas seized the chance to do something.

Innovation has three aspects: having a good idea; making it work; and demonstrating improvement. The first of these is the easiest: lots of people have good ideas all of the time; but making them work means encountering and overcoming not only the standard 50 British objections to change; but all manner of expected and unexpected resistances, not least of these the bewilderment of the client. The third component of innovation, proving that it works, is theoretically desirable but is almost always too costly or too time-consuming to be included in the innovator's plans. In a world of political decision-making any success which seems self-evident rarely awaits evaluation before application. Social scientists and planners may bewail this; but such is the characteristic fate of innovations.

Of the case studies in this book some are original

concepts; some are adapted from cognate fields; and others are copies of what has been done elsewhere. Some attracted strong support, others encountered powerful resistance. None was achieved without a struggle; and few turned out exactly as the innovator had envisaged. Almost all the innovations were based on the perceptions of the providers rather than of the receivers of care. This is how innovation seems to thrive. Desirable though it may appear to be, it is rare for clients to express their wishes directly. At the same time the perceptions of providers are strongly based on their close understanding of how the clients wish their needs to be met. Innovation, it appears, is paternalistic.

This is by no means a comprehensive account of all innovations in the care of the elderly, not even of all those known to us in the place and time of our study. It is selective and is concerned more with process than with outcome. It is hoped that those who have attempted to change a little bit of the world over which they exercise personal responsibility will derive from this account of the experience of others some insight, encouragement and incentive.

Chapter One

THE NATURE OF INNOVATION

Bernard Isaacs

An innovation has three components: a good idea, making it
work, and demonstrating that it works.

Good ideas are the products of inspiration, translation
or emulation.

Inspiration is an idea that has never been thought of before; translation is one taken from a quite different field;
and emulation is copying what has already been done.

Few are gifted with absolute originality and most of
these are astronomers or composers. The ability to translate
good ideas from other times, places and fields of activity is
a rare gift, requiring the vision of seeing what is similar in
different states and what is different in similar states.
Emulation is the Higher Plagiarism, necessitating the nice
mixture of humility and pride which is inherent in the phrase
'If they can do it' (a concession to their pre-eminence) 'then
so can we'(a re-statement of our own pre-eminence) .

Innovation is disruptive. It necessitates changes in the
way in which people work and think. It is not enough for the
innovator himself to see the Vision of the Brave New World
which his Idea will open up. He has to capture the minds of
those others who will, as a result of his innovation, be required to do a different job in a different way; to subject
cherished ideas to re-examination; to see new vistas not at
all as rosy as those of the Great Innovator.

Innovations usually cost money. When the innovations described in this volume were introduced cost did not dominate
quite so obtrusively as it does as this introduction is being
written, a time when infant innovations are strangled in their
cradles at the first whimper of more money having to be spent.

Innovation is in the public eye. Advantages must be made
plain to those who receive, deliver and pay for them. Rhe-
toric convinces some; but in every scene there are hard-
nosed men and women demanding hard facts and hard brass. The
most inspired schemes have their disadvantages, not all for-
seeable. The case must be worked out in much detail before
the innovation starts its journey through the bureaucratic

birth canal. It must fulfil its promises and early be shown
to do so.

THE CARE OF THE ELDERLY

Innovation grows best in Spring, when the soil is bare and the
climate is changing. Services for old people in the past were
bare enough, based as they were on parsimonious paternalism.
Old people were given what was best for them and they were
given it on the cheap. In today's warmer climate it is easy
to express the idea of replacing paternalism by respect for
human dignity and individuality. The innovator with imagination and experience of progress in other fields like the care
of children soon sees how to apply these principles to his
area of concern. Parsimony is not so easy to replace. The
innovator must either put something there that was not there
before, which is expensive; or remove something that was
there before, which is disruptive. Of the innovations to be
described here some actually demonstrated that they saved
money. Some, described in chapters four, ten and eleven,
managed to establish themselves without costing money. Others,
such as those described in chapters twelve and fourteen,
succeeded in finding new sources of money.

The care of the elderly in the past involved out-door relief, or cash handouts; in-door relief or institutionalisation; and a third element which Dorothy Wedderburn called
'The Myth of All Old People'; and which I refer to as the
metamorphosis principle. This states that after a certain age
and below a certain income the infinite variety of human nature clots into a formless mass; adult men and women meta-
morphose into 'old people' or 'the elderly' or 'senior citizens'; with attributes and needs which are characterised by
the years which they have attained rather than the years that
they have spent in attaining them. This fatuous view of old
people is no longer held by enlightened people (circular definition of 'enlightened') but even enlightened people use unenlightened words, like doctors who attribute symptoms of illness to 'your age'; or do unenlightened things, like archi-
tects who build homes with beautiful views of trees and flowers
when the occupants might prefer beautiful views of streets and
people.

Innovators seek to replace paternalism by participation,
homogeneity by individuality; and parsimony by public expenditure. They provide services which meet the needs of clients;
rather than seeking amongst the clients for needs which the
service can provide.

FROM PATERNALISM TO PARTICIPATION

The paternalistic attitude to old people stems from perception
of them as physically dependent, mentally obsolete, and objects

to be nice to. Many old people will accept this description
of themselves and obligingly complete a negative feedback loop.
The innovator breaks this by perceiving that dependence is but
a diminution of independence; obsolescence a product of dis-
use; and niceness a superior form of distancing. He learns
what old people want, not by distributing questionnaires, another form of distancing, but by rubbing up against them in
blunt proximity, with eyes and ears open. On learning that
they do not all want the same thing and most just want to be
left alone the innovator proposes the delicious but dangerous
change of letting old people off the leash. He then changes
his task from setting limits to the liberty of the ageing human spirit to setting limits to the damage that can result
from unbridled freedom. Examples of such innovations in this
book are the use of high rise flats for sheltered housing with
minimum disturbance of the residents, (Chapter Six);the maintenance of the mentally ill elderly at home with the help of a
Day Centre (Chapter Twelve);and the sharing of the care of the
severely impaired between hospital and home (Chapter Eleven).

FROM HOMOGENEITY TO INDIVIDUALITY

The difficulty of changing from an 'all old people' to an
'individual' approach is that no care provider believes that
he is not already practising an individual approach. The ag-
enda of social support begins with safety. With the limitation of 'safety first' a carer may genuinely believe that the
care offered provides individual choice. But that may be no
more than a choice between pudding and prunes as part of an un-
desired lunch at a table shared with strangers. Carers encourage individual choice, so long as the individual makes the
right choice. The innovator wants to give old people freedom
to make the wrong choice. The old person who should 'ideally'
be in an Old People's Home may choose not to be. The person
who should be clean, well fed and safe is allowed to be dirty,
scraggy and at risk. The innovator provides services to meet
either choice. His task is to convince the convinced that they
are not convinced,to explain that the banal principle of individuality has some startling implications. Many of the innovations described in this book accept these implications, and
contain the definition of 'acceptable risk' as the price to be
paid for individual freedom of choice.
    The reason that such an obvious lesson as 'old people are
individuals' has to be rehearsed again and again is that it is
simpler and cheaper to treat them as Biomass. If their needs
are all the same they can be batch processed on a production
line by few poorly trained and poorly paid staff with standar-
dised equipment. As soon as the principle of 'individual
choice' comes in, so too does data acquisition, programme planning, record keeping, decision making, consumer choice multi
disciplinary case conference, and a host of labour-intensive

education-intensive high-cost activities with dubious outcomes
and rampant professionalisation. Many of the most successful
'innovations' in the care of the elderly are essays in the removal of the chains with which a previous generation of beneficent innovators shackled the struggling individuality of old
people. Examples of these in this volume include the description of an enlightened home help service (see Chapter Five) and
the socialisation of aphasic stroke victims (see Chapter Eight).

FROM PARSIMONY TO PUBLIC EXPENDITURE

It seems a long time since the notion prevailed of caring for
old people at the lowest possible charge to the public purse;
but today's emphasis on cost effectiveness brings the idea back
in modern guise. The wily innovator exploits the difference in
outlook between economists and accountants. Economists talk
about 'opportunity costs' and 'marginal costs' which some members of public bodies may not fully understand. Innovators
should be able to produce evidence that their innovations will
make 'notional savings', which should at least be sufficient to
fund a 'pilot project'. Committee members are usually willing
to support 'pilot projects'; because they are seen to demonstrate the forward looking encouragement given to those with
new ideas, while at the same time reflecting a proper spirit
of prudence in the care of the public purse. The innovator
well knows that once a project is started and seen to be apparently doing good, any attempt to disband it will raise political outcries. By the time the accountant announces that the
'notional savings' are costing real money it is too late to
stop. The 'notional savings' in any case were only savings
when compared with a more expensive service which was not
being given away anyway.
 Those who have their houses painted and decorated know
that a better job costs more, and it is naive to pretend that
the same is not true of caring for old people. It is not a
matter of where the service is given but of how many people of
what degree of training are paid to give it. To replace nothing with something, or a little with a bit more costs money.
There remains an obligation on the innovator to see that the
money is well spent.
 The doctrine of 'cost-effectiveness' states that the objective is defined in advance; the extent to which it is attained is measured; and the costs of attaining it are calculated. The 'givens' are that the objective is worthy; that it
could not be attained by the expenditure of less money; or
that spending the same money in a different way could not
achieve other more appropriate objectives.
 It would be surprising if innovators gave more than a cur-
sory nod in the direction of these ideas. The concepts pose
questions which cannot be objectively answered (although there
are those who pretend to be able to answer them); because they

leave out of account the enthusiasm, conviction and dedication
which makes innovations work; and because measurement of effectiveness evaluates a 'movie' by examining a 'still'. The
innovative service does not stay the same for long enough for
a true picture to be taken of what it is doing. Innovations
change as new ideas become modified, routinised, and no longer
innovative. Comparison of the new with the old is contamina-
ted by the effect of novelty. If the innovation is no good it
is dropped; if it appears to be good it is replicated; and
subsequently comparisons have to be with areas which have not
had the initiative to modify their own service, so the comparison is questionable.

Many of the innovations described in this book have been
funded from new sources of money. Few have been formally evaluated. Some like the Stroke Scheme (Chapter Eight) are re-
plications of evaluated services from other parts of the country. Few services anywhere have been replicated because of the
findings of a cost-effectiveness study; and few have failed
to be replicated because of the absence of a cost-effectiveness
study. This may be deplored but not ignored. It seems to say
something about the nature of change in public service. It
may represent a gap in credibility, between scientific and evaluative research; or a difference in pace between political and
scientific imperatives; or the elusiveness of the object to be
measured. The spread of innovation in a politically visible
field, such as the care of the elderly, seems more suited to
the activities of the publicist than of the scientist. The innovator needs communication skills in so far as these are based
on objective data such as the number of clients dealt with by
a service or the unit cost. Crisp and clear presentation is at
least as useful as extensive documentation. But also required
is a flair for the telling anecdote, the evocative photograph,
the microphone and the camera. The change from public parsimony to public profligacy must gain public popularity.

CONCLUSION

The themes of this essay are extensively illustrated in the descriptions of practical achievements by practical people moving
two steps ahead of public opinion to provide new services in
new ways. These ways are sufficiently novel to be called 'in
novatory', but not so startling as to be called 'revolutionary'.
All the innovations have been preserved to become part of the
service to the public. Many have been replicated by the innovator or by another authority. All are being monitored and
modified with growing experience. They are altering the level
of expectation of old people of the services which they can receive; and they are altering the perceptions of old people
which are held by those who seek to serve them. They illustrate the vision and perseverance involved in creating innovations in the care of the elderly.

Chapter Two

PROMOTING INNOVATION - A DISTRICT MEDICAL OFFICER's VIEW

R. Griffiths

It is difficult to generalise about innovation because it involves a departure from what has gone before. Despite this it is helpful to classify the processes involved because it may facilitate new thinking.

The broadest taxonomy we could use in the health service context might be innovations for their own sake and innovations for the patients' sake. Some innovation for its own sake is probably essential, because it is difficult to accept that the world has reached a state of perfection which we must not change. However, this is damaging if it is carried too far. It is regrettably true that in medicine many new features of clinical practice or medical equipment are introduced for the professional satisfaction of the doctors concerned, even though they can be shown to have marginal or even harmful impact on patient care. The review of expensive medical techniques by the Council for Science and Society (1983) documents a number of instances of this sort of innovation. It is important that most health care professionals should be able to recognise this kind of change for what it is and make sure that it does no more than fulfil its legitimate role of maintaining professional interest without harming patients. The rest of this chapter will therefore be concerned with innovation for the patients' sake and how we may seek it, recognise it and foster it.

Innovation for the patients' sake must by definition be problem-oriented and must have gone through a number of recognisable stages: recognition of the problem; inspiration and hypothesis formation; experimentation and evaluation; and finally, implementation.

RECOGNITION OF THE PROBLEM

This stage of the innovative process is usually given inadequate attention. Very often problems are not clearly defined until an inspiration has come along which may solve part of it, and then the problem is defined in order to suit the

8

solution and often in order to justify investment in the solution which has become attractive in its own right. It is a surprisingly difficult thing for any group of staff to sit down and define what their current problems are; but any effective team should include within its normal routine a periodic assessment of its problems; whether they are clinical, administrative or personal.

When assessing a problem it is necessary to have a mental checklist which is very helpful in defining the kind of inspiration that is required, and which will provide a background to evaluation at a later stage. Most important, we should have a notion of how common the problem is, in formal terms what are the incidence and the prevalence? To put it another way, how often does this problem crop up and how long does it go on for once it has cropped up? This method can be applied to administrative problems just as easily as it can be to clinical ones. We can ask ourselves how often does the chest X-ray show an abnormality just as easily as we can ask ourselves how often do we fail to have the correct X-rays in outpatients? In either case we need to know whether the changes in the X-ray, whether they are changes in clinical appearance or losses to the system, are permanent or episodic, and we might need to know the proportion of patients to whom these changes apply. Some estimate of the incidence and prevalence is usually essential in deciding the priority of attack on a problem and in assessing the cost of any solution.

Another feature of our mental checklist is the size of the problem and the size of the change that is necessary to effect a solution. To continue the same example, do the patients show major changes in their lung function or merely minor discrepancies from normal; or on an administrative front do we lose all of the patients' X-rays or just some of them? Similarly, we can pose the characteristics of a useful solution in quantitative terms. Would a 50 per cent improvement in lung function make all the difference to the patient? Would finding 10 per cent more of the X-rays make all the difference to our function within a clinic?

Essential to each of these three estimates is a denominator, which is the last part of the checklist. We need to know the total population of patients, events or things within which our problem is found, as well as the proportion who have the problem and the relative size of the problem. It is the denominator that connects us to the real world. Without it we cannot make effective comparisons between one problem and another.

INSPIRATION AND HYPOTHESIS FORMATION

The mechanisms by which inspiration is created are probably impossible to describe. Inspiration is assisted by different

things in different people, and one should actively seek to be
aware of one's own particular pattern. Despite this individual variation, from the point of view of a team certain
things can facilitate the process. If a team recognises the
importance of inspiration, then apparently half-baked ideas
are not rejected out of hand but are carefully explored. It
is important that the team sets aside time at which problems
can be defined and redefined and progress checked. There
should be time for unstructured discussion as well as for careful review. When ideas are proposed, however trivial they may
appear, it is important to argue them through to their end
consequences and to try and estimate their impact upon particular problems. It is worth trying to define how long it
would take for a particular action to produce a noticeable
effect on the problem in hand. Inspiration and hypothesis
formation are not identical processes, and it is important to
progress from the first to the second. Only when an inspiration has been translated into a formalised hypothesis can one
proceed to the next phase of innovation which is experimentation and evaluation.

EXPERIMENTATION AND EVALUATION

This is probably the most important phase that any innovation
goes through, and it is often the one which is most neglected.
All too often, possible changes in clinical practice are evaluated only in terms of their technical competence as procedures rather than their intended effectiveness as elements of
a service. Probably the most notorious example of an effica-
cious procedure which has not been translated into an effective service is cervical cytology as a screening test for cervical cancer. For the last ten years two and a half million
smears per year have been taken and read in the UK, but the
mortality from the disease has fallen by less than 10 per cent
because the wrong women were screened. If the processes of
problem definition and hypothesis formation are carried out
properly, evaluation will be straightforward, because we will
know how often we expect to encounter the problem and what the
expected effect of the particular proposed solution will be.
Without these two crucial pieces of information an adequate
experiment is virtually impossible.

IMPLEMENTATION OF CHANGE

In order to examine implementation it is necessary to classify
the nature and type of changes that are proposed. Broadly
speaking they fall into three categories: revenue changes,
which are usually an alteration either in staffing levels or
in such things as drug costs or quantities of drugs prescribed;
capital changes, which are alterations in the fixed equipment
or buildings used to carry out a service; and behavioural

changes, which usually mean changes in the attitudes of those providing the service. Each of these methods of changing the provision of a service requires quite different approaches to implementation.

Although a great deal of attention is usually focused on the first two, it is the third, behavioural change, which is by far the most important. This paradox is explained if we examine the rate at which new revenue can produce change in the service as a whole. In the most beneficent of times the health service was able to grow at the rate of about 5 per cent of new resources per year, although ordinarily growth has been far less than this. If new resources come into a service at the rate of 5 per cent a year, it takes 20 years before these amount to half of the total that is being deployed. In other words, it takes approximately a professional lifetime to change half of the NHS, if one is relying entirely on new resources as the mechanism. Within individual parts of the service new revenue can produce more rapid changes but it is rare for revenue growth to be possible for several years in sequence. In the majority of services the amount of change created by new revenue over five to ten years is small.

Changes in capital resources allow much more rapid change, usually because they provide the opportunity for behavioural change. The provision of a new piece of equipment may allow all the existing staff to treat patients in a new way, so capital change is the next most effective.

Behavioural change, however, is possible simply by changing professional attitudes and the professional perception of the task. For instance, one of the most dramatic alterations in health service provision over the last 20 years was reduction in length of stay in hospital for most medical and surgical conditions, brought about by changes in professional attitudes. Changes in revenue and capital spending followed from it; they did not cause it.

It is paradoxical therefore that the mechanisms which allows us to create the greatest possible change in the organisation of services is the cheapest; that which allows the second most dramatic change, capital, is the easiest source of money to produce; and the most difficult source of money, new revenue, is likely to produce the least change in deployment of service. Far too much attention in the past has been focused on the addition of new revenue because, although it is hard to find, it is superficially easiest to plan. Now that this particular source of change has virtually dried up, we can begin to focus our attention on the other two mechanisms for changing the system, which are likely to be far more effective as a means of altering services.

PRODUCING BEHAVIOURAL CHANGE

If one is seeking behavioural change as a means of altering

services, then it is necessary to define the nature and size of the change that is required in behaviour and the target group whom one wishes to behave differently. Is the change confined to one professional discipline, or is alteration required in the behaviour of teams of people; or are a cluster of different behaviours required across a multi-disciplinary group? A clear understanding of the target group or groups is essential to any strategy for introducing change effectively.

Within a particular professional or occupational group formal and informal educational mechanisms are usually the most effective ways of producing change. These may be based on formal curricula, for instance, the introduction of new material into training courses; or continuing education through journals, research seminars, professional meetings and so on. In all these mechanisms the most important factor which determines whether or not a particular innovation is accepted is very often the power base from which it is proposed. This may be defined in terms of the professional credibility of those who propose it, combined with the academic or service credibility of the data and analysis upon which their proposals are based. It is unfortunately true, and probably always will be, that eminent men are often able to make proposals for action on the basis of very slight data, whereas women, or men of less eminence require much more data in order to persuade their colleagues. Although we may deplore this state of affairs, we have to take it into account if we seek to change the behaviour of our colleagues. An important initial step towards influencing the generality of people within the speciality may be the formation of suitable alliances and power bases of influential members of the profession concerned. It is not the purpose of this paper to discuss the ways in which innovations can be published or introduced into postgraduate or undergraduate curricula; but we should recognise that these are powerful ways of affecting the behaviour of our colleagues, and we should be prepared to explore their use in a systematic manner if we wish to change the way in which our patients are treated.

When change in the behaviour of multi-disciplinary groups is necessary a combination of techniques is often essential. Each professional discipline should be attacked by the educational means already mentioned; but within the health care institution itself there may be mechanisms available to influence the behaviour of our colleagues. Informally, most organisations support research groups, discussion groups and irregular meetings whose purpose is the stimulation of professional interest and development. These are frequently organised on a client group basis rather than a professional basis, and are one of the most obvious channels by which new innovations can be communicated to different staff and tested against their existing ideas.

More formally within the system most District Health Authorities rely on health care planning teams of a multi-disciplinary nature to advise on the development of services. In the past these teams have concentrated on preparing bids for changes in capital and revenue funding for the client groups under discussion. There is however no reason why health care planning teams should not address themselves to behavioural changes and recommend training schemes to acquaint staff with new techniques as part of the planning process of the Authority. In my own District, our Authority has already accepted the notion of seminars for Authority members provided by health care planning teams as a means of informing the members of the Health Authority about services for particular client groups.

Continuing education now plays a much more important part in professional development and progress up the various hierarchies. A considerable proportion of the additional education now necessary in order to gain promotion has little to do with the everyday life of the professionals concerned, a phenomenon well explained in Fred Hirsch's Social Limits to Growth. When we compete for positional goods, much of the competition is based upon unnecessary activity that does not move the entire community forwards. As Fred Hirsch says, when everyone stands on tiptoe no-one sees any better. Rather than despair of this continuing postgraduate explosion, we would do better to think carefully about the curricula content and try to use postgraduate education as a means of continuing to produce innovation and change within professional groups. The way things are at the moment there is a real danger that continuing postgraduate education produces the opposite effect, diverting excessive energy into the ritual incantation of professional creeds in churches far removed from patient contact.

Probably one of the most important prerequisites in producing behavioural change in an organisation is respect for the expertise and standing of our colleagues. If we take the trouble to be familiar with what our professional colleagues can and cannot do, we are far more likely to be able to secure their agreement to different ways of working. Almost all of us now work in teams, and for a team to be effective its members must respect each other. If teams wish to develop their activities in an effective and innovative manner they must be prepared to review their own performance continuously and to criticise each others' contribution constructively. The skills required in order to make teams function effectively in these ways are not inborn to all of us, but can be studied, practised and refined. Any team which wishes to provide a more effective service to its patients would be well advised to spend some time studying its own workings (Eskin, 1983, Chapter Four).

CAPITAL PLANNING

In this section by capital I mean money which is deployed once
only. When we consider the purchase of new buildings or new
equipment as a means of altering the service, we should be
thinking about the role that this new plant is going to play.
It is important to have some kind of classification in mind,
because it will influence our evaluation of the success of the
new plant and the sources of funding which could be available
to buy it. We need to decide whether the plant is to have a
general or a specific purpose. An example of general purpose
might be the purchase of a new type of bed or the addition of
more floor space; whereas a specific item might be the introduction of a new form of walking frame or a new surgical
technique, for some patients only. It is also important to
decide whether the equipment is supportive or therapeutic,
whether it will be used by all staff or only by selected
groups, and whether the equipment will be rate-limiting in any
way; will we need to make facilities available for coping
with a queue?

Most districts divide capital items into categories based
on the purpose and price. It is necessary to be familiar with
the local system. It is usual to separate buildings from
equipment and large items from small ones.

In recent years Joint Funding and the Inner City Partnership have brought capital money into the health service in
addition to that which is available through the main programmes.
Joint Funding was invented in the middle seventies in order to
allow the health service to speed up the implementation of
certain kinds of social service provision. The money is part
of the NHS budget but is to be spent on schemes in the community which are jointly approved by the Health Authority and
the local authority social service department. The original
circulars laid out fairly strict criteria for using this
money (DHSS 1977, 1979). The revenue cost of schemes must be
absorbed by the local authority or the NHS over a period of
time. This has considerably embarrassed many local authorities
and there has consequently been a tendency to divert much of
the Joint Funding allocation into capital schemes which have
small revenue consequences. A later circular changed the
rules to allow 100 per cent funding for ten years of schemes
designed to get patients out of hospital in certain fairly
tightly defined circumstances (DHSS 1983). It remains to be
seen what impact this new initiative will have on the Joint
Funding budget.

The Inner City Partnership is a partnership between the
central government and local authorities. A portion of the
money may be spent on health schemes. This proportion varies
considerably among the different local authorities to which
the scheme applies, so it pays to be familiar with the local
situation. The Inner City Partnership is governed by criteria

which lay down priorities and intended directions in which the
money should go. The revenue 'pick-up' mechanism is different
from joint funding. The Inner City Partnership normally provides 100 per cent of the funds for three years, following
which the Health Authority or the local authority has to pick
up the complete revenue cost. This has meant that the Inner
City Partnership has been used extensively for capital purposes. A number of health centres have been built in deprived
areas. It is possible to spend Inner City Partnership money
on hospital premises but it is difficult to provide hospital
schemes which meet the criteria of relevance to the health
problems associated with the deprivation that the populations
of the inner city suffer.

Most of these funds are problem-specific, in the sense
that they are additional monies voted by Parliament to deal
with some perceived difficulty faced by a population or institution. A clear definition of the problem is therefore essential in preparing a bid for money from any of these sources,
and in defining which of them may be able to help.

CHANGES IN REVENUE FUNDING

New long term revenue funding is the hardest thing to acquire
in the NHS, except in a District that is gaining significantly
from the Resource Allocation redistribution. (1) In any system where there is competition for scarce resources high
prices usually have to be paid for the goods concerned. In
the NHS the price is a prolonged battle through a bureaucratic
tangle. In many ways the planning system has become a system
of hurdles which any scheme must surmount if it is to be
first in line for what small amounts of money are available.
In many Districts even schemes at the top of the list remain
unfunded because the District is having resources removed in
order to put a little more money into more deprived areas.

The advice already given in this chapter should assist
with the process of battling through the planning system. Proposals should be problem-specific; they should say what proportion of the population they expect to influence; they
should say something of the size of the anticipated effect;
and the effect should be related to the cost. If planning is
done rationally, the notion of opportunity cost is probably
the most important. Stated quite simply, opportunity cost
means the things that we will not be able to do if we decide
to do the things that we do do. Opportunity costs have to be
compared across the various groups of patients that we are
trying to treat; and within the calculation we must take
account of the Government's declared priorities and of any instructions which the District Authorities may have obtained
from the Regional Health Authorities. Within that framework
the District Health Authority will have to determine its priorities. Hopefully, these will be based upon a rational

assessment of the health of the community for which the
Authority is responsible.

In addition to the rational planning system, there is
also an irrational one. The process of deciding so-called
priorities must be based upon value judgements, which in the
end are political. It is important therefore not only to make
out an appropriate rational case but to make sure that the
lobbying has been done in order to secure the political power
base which will vote the particular areas of concern to the top
of the priority list.

While politics alone will not suffice to get poorly
thought-out plans funded, it is also true that brilliant plans
are unlikely to be funded if the political homework has been
left undone.

Because new revenue in the mainstream funding is so
scarce it is important to make every possible effort to make
the best use of existing resources. Any unit, no matter what
client group it is treating, should examine very carefully the
cost of its existing methods of working and try to see whether
there are ways of carrying out the same task for less money.
This is the same as saying that behavioural change is more
likely to be effective than seeking new revenue. As Rutherford
said, 'We have no money, therefore we must think'. The same
criterion applies to Inner City Partnership and Joint Funding
monies which, because of the embarrassment of the long term
revenue 'pick-up', will always be harder to obtain for revenue
schemes than for capital, although the rules remain essentially
the same as those described in the preceding section.

CRASHING THE SYSTEM

Having said all this about the system as it is intended to
work, it is obvious to anyone who studies the health service
that some individuals repeatedly try to crash the system.
There are two main methods by which this is done. The first
is deliberate overspending. This is easiest in those areas
which are hardest to monitor, for instance drug costs; and
most difficult in those which are easiest to monitor, namely
manpower levels. Even here, the judicious use of locums and
careful manipulation of Whitley Council regradings may enable
the revenue budget of a particular department to be built up in
a way which allows the Health Authority little control over
the process. The other recognised system is direct appeal to
the public via the newspapers, in order to raise political
pressure, or to raise money through a charitable appeal for a
particularly attractive piece of equipment or mechanism for
some startling new 'break-through'. Both of these tactics are
effective in the short term, in that they frequently attract
money into a particular area over and above that which should
have been provided in the year in question. The money can only
be found, of course, by taking it from other departments who

have been less strident in their methods. (Even charities admit that they are competing within a finite pool which can be suddenly depleted by such things as appeals in response to national or international diasters.) It is often possible by means of 'charitable blackmail' to persuade Authorities to provide revenue funds, in order to make operational pieces of capital equipment which have been paid for by charitable funds.

These well known tactics are described in the Council for Science and Society's booklet Expensive Medical Techniques. In the the long run they lead to anarchy in the system, to disruption of the normal medical advisory machinery, and to the annoyance or anger of colleagues. If pursued too far, they may compromise the ability of a particular consultant to obtain effective resources for his patients, because he may build up such a level of resentment that legitimate calls for money are ignored. Most Authorities now have committees to approve fund raising appeals. While these may appear to be yet another set of bureaucratic controls they allow the possibility of co-ordinating popular fund raising with rational planning. If the Authority approves a project in advance and guarantees long-term revenue funding, it often makes the appeal more attractive for support from newspapers and the public.

In summary, then, you can crash the system, you can ignore your colleagues, but if you do so, you can be assured that any competent community physician will see you coming, unless of course you find some new and particularly innovative way of beating the system.

MAINTAINING OPTIMISM

Within the organisation optimism is important. Just as a team must encourage its members so must a Health Authority. This is difficult when finances are restricted, so it is important that specific measures are taken to encourage innovation. First of all, suggestions for saving should be rewarded. The simplest way of doing this is by allowing those responsible to retain part of the savings for redeployment within their own areas of activity. When times are especially hard this may be possible only on a non-recurrent basis, but the principle is worth pressing for whenever money is restricted.

The second important measure is to make sure that some funds are set aside for research and evaluation. Too often research means trying new additional measures, but those responsible for allocating funds can also encourage enquiry into the effectiveness of services and into the testing of alternative methods of providing services.

As we noted in the introduction some change is necessary in order to ensure that job satisfaction and creativity are encouraged. Perhaps it is a paradox to end the chapter by saying that some innovation for its own sake is essential from the patient's point of view. This is true because, without an assurance that change is possible, thinking stagnates. On the other hand we cannot encourage innovation in an entirely un-critical way. From the organisation's point of view it is a fine line to tread; and the safest path is to ensure that a sum is always set aside for evaluation of services. This at least guarantees that innovative thinking can be encouraged at the same time as providing the opportunity for better services. This maintains optimism which is essential because, in the words of Peter Ustinov, 'Life is far too serious for pessimism'.

NOTE

1. See: Department of Health and Social Security Sharing Resources for Health in England: Report of the Resource Allocation Working Party, published by HMSO, 1976, which sets out a method of calculating a target level of resources for each region. Most regions have applied a similar formula to arrive at a target resource level for each district and where this differs significantly from a level of funding arrived at by applying current inflation rates to historic levels of re-source allocation, regions are pursuing a policy of realloca-tion to those who are below target and removal of resources from those that are above target.

REFERENCES

Council for Science and Society (1983) Expensive medical techniques: Report of a Working Party, CSS, London
Department of Health and Social Security (1977) Circular HC(77)17, DHSS, London
Department of Health and Social Security (1979) Circular HC(79)18, DHSS, London
Department of Health and Social Security (1983) Circular HC(83)6, DHSS, London
Eskin, F. (1983) Doctors and management skills, MCB Publica-tions, Bradford
Hirsch, F. (1977) Social limits to growth, Routledge & Kegan Paul, London
Ustinov, P. (1980) Happiness, Baggs Memorial Lecture, University of Birmingham

Chapter Three

HOW LOCAL GOVERNMENT FUNDS INNOVATIONS IN SOCIAL SERVICES

R. Liddiard

INTRODUCTION

Social Service Departments of Metropolitan Districts, such as the City of Birmingham, of shire counties and of London boroughs are charged by central government with the responsibility of funding a range of mandatory and optional services for dependent client groups. Traditionally children formed the major group in need of social services, but in recent years the elderly, along with the mentally ill, the physically handicapped and the mentally handicapped have emerged as priority groups with powerful claims on the attention of Departments.
    In order to meet these new needs local authorities had to expand, modify and adapt their services. 'Innovation' has become their way of life. In this chapter a description will be given of the organisational and financial background against which innovation has taken place. Some aspects of the innovative process will be outlined, and the obstacles to innovation discussed. Some of the major innovations stemming from this Department are described elsewhere in this volume. Further examples of smaller-scale innovations will be presented here.

THE BACKGROUND

Local authorities are theoretically independent of central government, although in practice they are severely constrained by legislation, by government financial policy and by the fact that they receive more than half their income from central government. The personal social services continue within local control. This produces variety and local ingenuity, but also wide variation in type, standards and quality of service.
    There are three systems, all reporting to the Secretary of State for Social ISecurity. The system of social services is directly funded and directly managed by central government. The personal social services system is indirectly funded and locally managed; while the health service is directly funded and indirectly managed. These three systems have separate

hierarchies, recruitment, training and traditions. It would be difficult to devise an organisation which had more potential problems. However, it is remarkable how closely the systems can work together when the local personnel set out to achieve that goal.

Of the three systems, social services is the most independent. As part of local government, its policies, financing and planning depend on its being separate from central government, although it remains subject to audit, advice and, in extreme circumstances, direction by central government. This tradition is normally upheld by central government which intervenes only exceptionally, but which constantly encourages and cajoles local authorities, whilst retaining its inspectorial powers for circumstances which require them.

Much of the legislation governing the operation of social services departments is discretionary in the sense that, whilst services must be provided for those with particular needs, the local authority is responsible for determining whether the need exists. There are minimum statutory requirements which are codified in legislation concerning children and young persons. Some legislation concerning the elderly, the disabled, the chronically sick and the mentally disordered is also compulsory, but the required degree of implementation is prescribed only in vague terms. This leaves much room for local variation in the extent and nature of services.

Local authorities have interpreted their responsibilities differently, so that services vary up and down the country and between types of authorities. These differences are attributable to the physical environment, the nature of the population, the way services are organised, the type of authority concerned, the relative wealth of the area, and the local political tradition. For example, inner London boroughs do not operate education services which are normally the largest spenders in local government and which elsewhere compete for resources with social services departments. Some departments found themselves forced into becoming largely child care organisations; and social work for the elderly, the mentally disordered, the chronically sick and the disabled was provided only or mainly in the form of emergency intervention. Policies have been subject to political decisions made both nationally and locally. A service which was provided in one year might be withdrawn, increased or reduced in the next, because of a change in political control leading to new ordering of priorities. A change in the financial situation might also affect social policy. For example, as a result of the drastic curtailment of local government expenditure in the late 1970s and early 1980s new initiatives were severely restrained unless existing services were curtailed or more cost-effective methods were devised.

FINANCE

Local authorities traditionally finance their social service programme from the locally levied rates and from grants from central government. Two additional sources of funding have been made available to encourage and support innovation – the Joint Financing and the Urban Aid Programmes. Yet there are severe limitations on how these services can be used, and these will now be discussed.

Joint Financing

In 1976 central government, aware of the difficulties experienced by local authorities in maintaining and expanding community services for the elderly, the mentally ill, the physically and mentally handicapped and children, introduced new financial arrangements. These allowed funds, which had been provided by Parliament for the health service, to be used by local authorities for projects which would enable the patients to remain in the community, thus benefiting the health services. The management of the funds was entrusted to a Joint Consultative Committee, composed of equal numbers of representatives of the local authority and, originally, the area health authority (since 1982 the district health authority).

In 1983/4 the health service contributed £1m and the local authority £800,000 to joint-funded projects. For the same year, the budget of the Social Services Department was £60m.

Local joint consultative committees supported by joint care planning teams of officers have a primary function of enabling joint planning to take place between the authorities. However, they have tended to concentrate on the spending of this money, rather than on the joint planning of their services.

The success of joint financing programmes has varied considerably between localities because of different political views, the degree of commitment of administrators and professionals, and the complexities of the differing financial systems operated by the health service and local authorities.

Inner City Partnership

Certain large cities including Birmingham have had the benefit of government funds aimed at deprivation in their inner areas. These so-called Partnership or Programme Areas have received 75 per cent funding for projects agreed jointly by central government; local authority, health authority and voluntary organisations.

Though the partnership programme is broad-based, a major proportion of its resources has been directed to economic and housing concerns. Health and personal services have received only a minor proportion of the finance available, although the balance is slowly changing.

A special effort is made to encourage self-help and

innovation. The difficulty is that schemes for personal social services usually involve employing people, with continuing financial commitments. The programme is orientated towards capital schemes which release funds for further schemes,
and many worthwhile revenue-based schemes do not proceed.
'Topic groups' have been set up, each dealing with a part of
the programme – for example health and personal social services, economy, housing – and this has the benefit of bringing
together various agencies; central, local and voluntary.

DIFFICULTIES IN LONG-TERM FUNDING

Both joint financing and the inner city partnership rely on
the local authorities eventually financing the projects directly themselves. The assumption, therefore, is of continued
growth in expenditure, whereas the strategy of central government is to reduce local government revenue spending.

Central government limits the expenditure of local authorities, although the local authorities may be willing to undertake additional expenditure. Thus, it is difficult for local
government to utilise special government spending programmes
without either future increases in revenue costs or a corre-
sponding reduction in other services in order to accommodate
the cost of new projects generated by special funding.

Local capital expenditure is not financed by cash grants.
The local authority merely has permission to borrow a certain
amount which has to be repaid over a period, usually up to 60
years. The repayment of capital loans has revenue consequences. New projects need staff to operate them and incur
other costs. Capital investment almost always needs revenue
cash to support the subsequent operating costs, inflated by
the loan repayments which may account for over half the expenditure.

Both central and local government budget on a year-by-
year basis. Local authorities may not know until very late in
their budgetary cycle what degree of support they will receive
from central government. It is therefore very difficult to
plan for a number of years ahead.

In local authorities with a volatile political situation
control may swing year-by-year from one political party to
another. Short-term political advantage may determine programmes being changed or developed, sometimes without much
apparent thought to the longer-term consequences. There is a
tendency for political leaders to concentrate either on the
basic services which cannot readily be changed or on projects
which look likely to catch votes – even though they are not
necessarily the most important developments from a longer-term
perspective.

The funding of programmes delivered through voluntary
organisations suffers. The local authority may be unable to
give long-term guarantees because it is not sure of its own

source of finance. Otherwise the local authority might have
to restrict its own services in order to maintain projects in
the voluntary sector.

INNOVATIONS

Despite these difficulties innovations have proceeded. In
addition to those described in chapters five, twelve and thirteen, the following examples can be cited.
      Projects may emerge from grass roots level, such as a
'Shared Care' scheme to provide foster care for mentally handicapped persons on a temporary basis while their families take
a rest. Similarly, a 'home from home' scheme was instituted
to give old people a break from their families and their families a break from them, by recruiting short-term 'substitute
families'. These schemes are worthy of wider application.
They are not new in themselves but they exemplify the value
of spreading good ideas.
      Birmingham is now thinking of making 'innovation budgets'
available at local level, albeit on a very small scale. A
start has been made by allowing local officials to give 'seed'
money to voluntary organisations in their area. The Director
of Social Services has a small grants scheme which enables
him to assist in a similar way.
      Local authorities are not organised so as to facilitate
innovation to the maximum degree. However, neither is the
converse true. A number of good ideas have been brought forward and developed, many of them in minor but significant
areas of work. Taken together they represent a steady and
gradual development of services which represent the realisation of ideas built into legislation during this century.
Constructive 'blurring' of the traditional boundaries of
professional disciplines and of the relationships between
professionals and elected members creates an atmosphere in
which good ideas can be developed, although not as rapidly as
one would like. Such innovation represents the best tradition of British local government.

Chapter Four

EARLY INTERVENTION IN A GENERAL PRACTICE

L. A. Pike

General practitioners are independent contractors – that is they operate within a framework of regulations but have a freedom of action denied to those who work in the hospital, community or social services. The price for this freedom of action is that the service provided to patients is dependent to a great extent on the financial input and personal effort of individual general practitioners, and the service is therefore uneven. The benefit of freedom of action is that innovation is always possible, being dependent on the individual GP and not on the machinations or manipulations of committees; although if the innovation requires the deployment of other members of the primary care team, then the GP will find himself involved in decision-making processes with the district health authority.

There are 23,000 GPs in England and Wales with an average list size of about 2,100 patients. Payments for services are complex but are based on the capitation fee which increases with the age of the patient. The basic fee for those under the age of 65 was in 1982 £5.30; for those aged 65-74 it was £6.85; and for those aged 75 and over £8.45. The differential payment is a recognition that elderly patients cause a greater work load. Patients aged 65 and over give three times more work than do those aged 16-64. They need more home visits, more consultations in the practice premises and more attention in every way. Most of the elderly confused patients are looked after at home by the primary care team and this group adds considerably to the GP's working time. Whereas in most areas 14 per cent or fewer of the patients are aged 65 and over, in retirement areas 20 per cent or more of the population may be in this age group. The problems created by the ageing population for GPs, hospitals and social services are similar in all areas since class disadvantages in health become less extreme as people grow older, and since death becomes more likely simply because of old age.

CONCEPTS OF CARE

The type of care given to the practice population by the general practitioner depends on his attitude to what 'care' is. It can be just dealing with crises as they arrive on his doorstep, or there can be a more preventive approach. My own concept of care is best demonstrated by thinking of an iceberg (Figure 4.1), two fifths of which lies above and three fifths below the surface.

Figure 4.1:

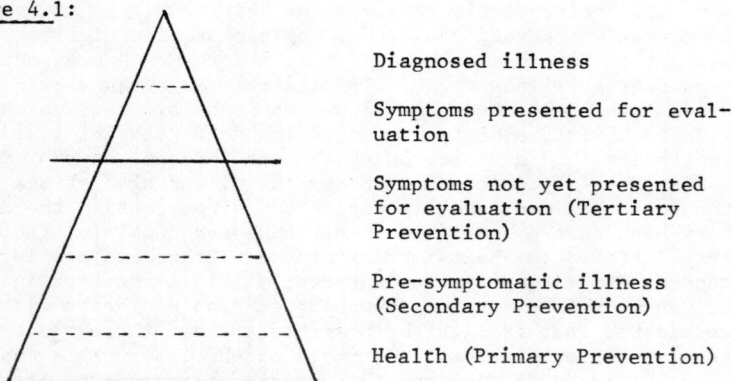

Diagnosed illness

Symptoms presented for evaluation

Symptoms not yet presented for evaluation (Tertiary Prevention)

Pre-symptomatic illness (Secondary Prevention)

Health (Primary Prevention)

Above the surface are those patients who have presented their symptoms to the doctor, and who have either been diagnosed as suffering from an illness or who remain, as yet, undiagnosed. Below the surface are those who have not yet presented their symptoms for diagnosis. This situation can be exemplified by a man bleeding from the anus who believes that the bleeding is due to piles and who is treating himself with suppositories which he has purchased from a pharmacy. The bleeding may, of course, be due to piles; but it might also be due to infection or to a cancer of the rectum. To avail himself of early treatment he should consult his doctor.

Below this layer are people who appear completely healthy and have no symptoms, but in whom clinical examination or special tests will reveal a problem. An example could be a woman with positive cervical cytology on testing who needs urgent referral to a gynaecologist. The lowest layer are those who have no complaints and who are normal on testing. Prevention of illness is still a possibility by health teaching, by immunisation and by such procedures as genetic counselling. I believe that it is possible to apply such a concept of care to the elderly in the practice.

GROWTH OF THE IDEA

Faced with increasing numbers of elderly people, an increasing

work load and a lessening proportion of the gross national
product being spent on the health services, what can GPs do?
They cannot rely on receiving increased services from hospitals or social services when their elderly patients become ill,
because there is little evidence of increasing resource allocation to provide for the growing numbers of elderly people.
Fortunately, the GP can restrict his horizons to those who are
on his list. Ten years ago I began to think how best to organise the care of our elderly population. I was aware of the
difficulties of arranging care in an emergency for an old person, which often led to the patient being admitted to hospital
when what was needed was urgent deployment of domiciliary
support to keep him at home. It seemed to me that a review of
resources available to elderly patients, in advance of urgent
need, might help when provision of home help, meals on wheels,
aids to living, aids to communication such as hearing aids or
spectacles, and district nurse support, becomes warranted in
the event of deterioration in health. I was also struck by
the fact that many elderly patients did not consult the doctor, because they attributed any and every complaint from which
they suffered to their increasing age. Other old people attended very frequently for apparently trivial matters and were
evidently not having some unmentioned problems dealt with. I
considered that it might be possible to meet these needs by a
regular review of elderly patients on our list. This was to
be achieved by sending the patient an appointment to attend at
a special session outside the normal consultation hours but
during the regular working day. Careful planning was needed
before beginning to operate such a session.

THE SETTING UP OF THE CLINIC

It was important to define the objectives of the clinic before
launching it into operation. I did not assume that a large
number of treatable medical conditions would be discovered at
the clinic, although there would be such conditions as diabetes, cancer of the breast and prostate which, if detected
early, might lead to a more comfortable life span if not a
lengthened one. The main objectives were defined as follows:

  1. To detect symptomatic and presymptomatic illness
     which is capable of treatment.
  2. To discover unmet medical and social needs and to
     try to remedy these needs.
  3. To improve communication between the patient and the
     members of the primary care team and to make the pa-
     tients aware of the roles of the team members.

If these objectives were to be attained, it would mean assem-
bling the members of the primary care team on the practice premises during a working day. It would mean sending invitations

to those aged 65 and over on our list; asking them to go for
a chest X-ray one week before attending the session; designing a questionnaire for them to complete prior to attending
(Appendix B); asking them to bring a urine sample to the
clinic; finding any way other than letter post as far as
possible, to despatch the invitations and the questionnaire;
and designing a problem sheet on which team members would record discovered problems and plan remedial measures. I had
also to think of the procedures to be carried out during the
examination, since tests are limited by their usefulness in
helping to achieve the objectives, by their acceptance by the
patient and by the time available to each individual at the
clinic. A good deal of time is saved by the questionnaire
and the chest X-ray prior to the examination.

Putting such a procedure into operation depends on all
the partners in the practice being convinced of the value of
the preventive approach to care of the elderly. Whilst I am
carrying out the examinations at the clinic, my partners will
be undertaking the routine work of general practice including
home visits. It also means that other members of the primary
care teams must be willing to organise their day to attend
the clinic.

THE PROCEDURE

The key to such an exercise is the age/sex register of the
practice. Every patient in the practice has a card made out
for this register on which is recorded full name, address and
post code, date of birth, and date joined, or left, the practice. These cards are filed by year of birth, so that it is a
simple procedure to make a nominal roll of those aged 65 and
over to be sent for. The register can also be used to record
who has attended the clinic, and I have introduced a coloured
sticker to attach to the cards of all those who have attended
for screening.

A photocopier enables the rapid production of stationery
such as letters and questionnaires. Various methods of delivering the invitations have been adopted, including using
the health visitor, doctor and nurse on home visits; keeping
a nominal roll of those to be sent for at the reception desk
and giving out the invitations when patients attend for some
other reason. However, a proportion of the letters have to
be posted. Initially we posted the invitations with a tear-
off slip for the patient to respond, but found that the sense
of timelessness which some patients exhibited frustrated the
efforts of an efficient scheme! One patient responded to the
invitation two years after receiving it. I now send a definite time for an appointment and ask the patient to let us
know if he is not going to attend.

Another problem is what to call the clinic. Certain
words such as geriatric, elderly, pensioners, are likely to

introduce negative reactions in the over 65s, and yet the session has to be given a name of some scrt. The letter which is sent out is reproduced in Appendix A. I hoped that this phraseology would not antagonise the patients and it has proved acceptable.

It is necessary to define in advance what procedures will be carried out by each team member. After consultation we aggreed our responsibilities as follows:

Practice Receptionist. She welcomes the patient and attaches the questionnaire, the problem sheet and the X-ray report to the ordinary medical record envelope.

Practice Nurse. She weighs and measures the patient; checks the need for chiropody; carries out an audiogram; tests the patient's eye sight using the Snellen test card, with the patient wearing his spectacles, if any; and tests the urine for albumen and sugar. I had hoped to use the attached health authority nurse in this role, but because of staff shortages, had eventually to appoint a practice nurse to carry out this work.

Health Visitor. She reviews the questionnaire (Appendix A) dealing with those questions which are particularly her responsibility. She identifies herself as the carer who has most to do with social problems such as housing, finance, recreational groups and holidays. She identifies those who could help the patient at times of sickness, notes their addresses and telephone number, and gives the patient her card with her name, practice address and telephone number. She presents the practice booklet, 'Health for the over 65s', and draws the attention of the patient to any relevant parts of the booklet. She carries out a ten-point test of mental function.

Laboratory Technician. I have been fortunate in having a technician who comes to the practice to carry out haematological and biochemical tests as part of a research project. Using the multi-channel autoanalyser, a full profile is produced within a week and is attached to the patients' notes for review with the other findings. Were we not to have this facility my choice of screening blood tests, to be carried out by our local laboratory, would be a full blood count, ESR, blood glucose and serum thyroxine. In my opinion, the majority of treatable illnesses which are as yet undiagnosed would be revealed by these tests.

General Practitioner. The patient is welcomed by the doctor and told that, in the event of any problem being uncovered, he will be asked to return by appointment for assessment in the light of the findings. Otherwise he will be told that no problem has been detected. He is told that there is no once-for-all screening, and that he will be recalled at intervals during his lifetime (or the doctor's!) for reassessment. He is also encouraged to present any subsequent departure from what he would regard as normal as soon as possible to the doctor for evaluation.

The doctor then checks the blood pressure, examines the eyes and the ears using the ophthalmoscope and auriscope, carries out a peak flow rate test with the flowmeter, reviews the questionnaire and carries out any examination that is indicated. For example, bleeding from the rectum demands a rectal examination and proctoscopy. The doctor pays particular attention to the first question on the questionnaire, 'Have you any health problems you wish to discuss with the doctor?', and carefully reviews any drug therapy - self-purchased and/or prescribed medicines. Finally, the need for dentures or dental treatment is noted.

Numbers
There are more than 7000 patients on the list, of whom about 850 are aged 65 and over. One hundred and seventy of these are in welfare homes for the elderly and are reviewed there annually, leaving 680 to be considered. Of these, about 250 are already under surveillance by the practice or hospital, so that we need to consider 430 for examination. We can cope with about ten patients per morning, so allowing for staff holidays we can screen the practice population aged 65 and over within about a year.

WHAT HAS BEEN ACHIEVED BY THE PROGRAMME?

It is possible to quantify the numbers of patients who are examined in a year, the new problems discovered and the attempts made to solve them; but it is much more difficult to quantify patient satisfaction and the attitudes of the team to the programme. Despite this, I would put at the top of the positive results the benefit to the relationship between the patient and the health care team, in particular the general practitioner. It is a source of satisfaction and appreciation of the work of the team that an effort has been made to invite a man or woman who probably has no medical complaints at the time of the invitation, to come to the medical centre for a check-up; to raise medical or social problems for discussion; and to answer a questionnaire which reviews aspects of his health or well-being; and to have a number of simple tests.

However, an attempt must be made to evaluate the other aspects of the programme. In one year, of a total of 855 patients, 76 per cent were screened or were already under surveillance, 6 per cent refused the offer of screening and 18 per cent were untraceable. This last group did not reply to our invitation and could not be traced by letter or subsequent visit. Those who did not attend were visited by members of the team to ascertain whether any problem existed, although no attempt was made to berate the patient over his non-attendance! The number subjected to full screening diminished as age increased. For example, only 30 per cent of the men aged 80 years or more were screened, but 53 per cent of this group were already under surveillance. Forty-five per cent of the 65-year-old men were screened while 20 per cent were already under surveillance. Similar patterns existed for the female population. Those who did not attend the clinic included people still at work; independent isolated people who did not want to subject themselves to examination; and those who were concerned that some serious problem might be discovered during the examination.

Of those screened, four categories were identified and classified as follows:

1. Those with definite problems at first test.
2. Those with a problem identified at the first test which was expected to cause trouble later.
3. Those with an abnormality not expected to produce a problem.
4. Those with no abnormalities.

1: 'Definite problems'. Any condition likely to make life difficult for the patient was classified as a 'definite problem'. Thus deafness requiring a hearing aid or ear syringing, mental illness, anaemia (less than 10.9 grams/100 ml), the need for chiropody, arthritis, temporal arteritis, severe obesity (> 25 per cent above average weight), skin disease, visual defects, and social problems were classified in this way.

2: 'Predicted problems'. Any condition considered to affect the quality of life of the patient in the foreseeable future was classified as a 'predicted' problem. In this category were moderate obesity (> 15 per cent but below 25 per cent above average weight); slight cardiac enlargement on X-ray; slight anaemia (between 10.9 and 11.9 grams/100 ml); tremor; haemorrhoids; some social needs; and need for eye refraction.

3: Other abnormalities. Other abnormalities discovered which were not likely to affect the quality of life in the foreseeable future were placed in the third category of 'abnormality but no anticipated problem'. Deafness in one ear, hyperuricaemia, some lung pathology, i.e. calcified glands or chronic bronchitis, and skin diseases were placed in this category.

Findings
Half the patients had a problem to discuss, the commonest being pain or weakness in joints, visual disorders and gastrointestinal upsets such as indigestion and constipation.

Table 4.1:   Problems detected in 465 patients aged 65
              and over on first clinic attendance

	Number
Total patients examined	465
Definite problem	104*
Predicted problem	96
Abnormal but no problem	41
No problem	237

*40 dealt with by health visitor

The number of patients in each category is given in Table 4.2,
and the outcome of the problems by second examination in Table
4.3.

Table 4.2:   First Test Abnormalities

Type of problem	Number of patients (percentage)
Definite problem	60 (43.2)
Predicted problem	45 (32.6)
Abnormality but no anticipated problem	7 (5.1)
No abnormality	26 (18.8)
Total	138 (100)

Table 4.3:   Outcome by Second Test (Percentages in Brackets)

	Number	Cured	Ameliorated	Unchanged
Definite problem	60 (100)	17 (28.3)	29 (48.3)	14 (23.3)
Anticipated problem	45 (100)	12 (25.6)	18 (40.0)	15 (33.3)
Abnormality but no problem anticipated	7 (100)	1 (14.3)	2 (28.6)	4 (57.1)
No abnormality	26 (100)	-	-	-

Since the population is examined at regular intervals the
number of problems diminishes with each examination, but new
problems are discovered. There is also a tendency for more social problems to be discovered once the patients realise the
possibility of a solution by health visitor intervention.
    An example of a patient with a 'definite' problem was a
man of 66 who had a painless ulcer of his scrotum which had

been present for six months. He mentioned this as a problem on his questionnaire, and subsequent referral to hospital confirmed the diagnosis of cancer which was treated successfully. An example of a 'predicted' problem was a man whose blood test revealed the possibility of alcohol abuse. He drank 20 pints of beer at the weekend and he was surprised to be told that this was a medical problem. He is being examined at regular intervals with his consent. An example of a patient with an abnormality, but no problem, was a lady with a loud heart murmur due to calcification of her aortic heart value, but no symptoms.

Most of the problems were capable of solution, though some patients were advised to obtain a solution by the expenditure of money. In Birmingham, the NHS is incapable of providing hearing aids in less than three years waiting time, and the waiting times for cataract extraction or dermatological consultations are almost beyond the expectation of life of some patients. My approach is to manipulate the system to the best of my ability for the benefit of my patients, but where this proves impossible to recommend the patient to buy whatever they need from the private sector, using charitable funds when the money is not available from their own resources.

Some problems are incapable of solution. I still regret the referral of an 88 year old lady with a breast tumour for surgery, who then suffered a pulmonary embolus after the operation and died. I now assume responsibility at times for a policy of intentional non-referral of such problems, although I undertake the continuing care of the unreferred.

EVALUATION

The cost of the clinic to the health service is negligible, allowing for the fact that the programme is part of the day-to-day work of the nurses, health visitor and doctor. The doctor pays for postage, stationery and premises for which he then claims tax relief. The cost of the laboratory techniques and the laboratory time is probably in the region of £5 per patient: a luxury which could be omitted, though this would be to the detriment of the patient and the team.

It must be said that prevention is not a soft option in terms of cost benefit. If prevention is successful and a patient lives longer, then he will cost the state more in social security benefits than if he were to die prematurely. Keeping an old person out of hospital saves expensive hospital costs, but requires costly supportive services at home.

In terms of reduction of workload, again, the team spend their time in a different way from ordinary contacts with patients. We have some evidence that our consultation rate for the elderly is less than in some other practices in more favourable areas.

Objections can be levelled at such a scheme of

anticipatory care. It is difficult to quantify the benefits in terms of the quality of the patient's life, the appreciation of the service by the patient, and the job satisfaction of the doctor; yet the reader must accept that these benefits do exist. The improved relationship between doctor and patient is invaluable.

Even so, it is possible to refute the critics who say that screening of healthy individuals is a waste of time. In 43 per cent of the screened population in 1981/2, most of whom considered themselves healthy, a predictable or an actual problem was found which had not been presented during routine consultations. Table 4.3 shows how many such problems are cured or ameliorated. I am not saying that there are not alternative ways of dealing with the problems, but for me, this seems the most appropriate and the most rewarding one.

THE FUTURE

I have detailed a simple programme of health surveillance and prevention for our older patients in this practice. The benefits for our partnership have been considerable, and we will continue the process, certainly whilst I am in practice. It is possible for any general practitioner to institute such a programme, or any other programme he may care to devise. Primary care is at the frontier of health care. There are more and more older people, with severely limited resources for their care. It seems to me that the primary care team must bear the brunt of the problems of an ageing population. Practical measures which would advance the care of the elderly include the provision of freepost facilities for doctor/patient consultations; the more readily available attachment of health visitors and nurses to primary care teams; financial help for GPs to set up age/sex registers; and increased remuneration for caring for the elderly.

My recommendation to other general practitioners who might be considering extending their programme of care for the elderly would be to look at their own situation, look for sources of help from their colleagues, from their nurses and health visitors, and define objectives. My solution may not be best for others, but it provides a framework for comparison.

POSTSCRIPT

Probably the first attempts to discover medical needs in the elderly population in the UK was the report from Williamson et al, 'Old People at Home: their unreported needs'. In this survey local authority health visitors, working with the co-operation of several general practitioners in Edinburgh, visited patients in their own home, and then invited them to attend a consultation at a hospital geriatric clinic.

Elliott and Stevenson (1973) reviewed the literature on

geriatric care in general practice, and offered definitions of problems and possible solutions rather than an account of actual schemes. Howe (1973) described a team approach to caring for the elderly at home.

Freedman et al (1978), from Newcastle, described a method of screening the elderly population in their practices using area health authority personnel, but were concerned with the detection of serious treatable illness, and reported that there was little treatable but previously undiagnosed illness within the community studied.

Barber and Wallis (1978) reported a fall in problems detected between two screening examinations of a Health Centre population in Glasgow and stated that they remained convinced that a continuing programme of geriatric assessment is valuable.

Gert Almind (1983) from Copenhagen gave the results of a review carried out by three GPs - himself, Charles Freer from Ann Arbor in Michigan, Gregg Wishaw from Durban, N. Carolina and a community physician, J. A. Muir Gray from Oxford. Of the GPs contributing to the care of the elderly they propose a check list for every primary care team to ask itself:

1. Could I meet the needs of the whole population of elderly people more effectively than I am doing at present?
2. Could I take the views of elderly people and their relatives into account to a greater extent in the scheduling of office hours, in the way we receive 'phone calls or in other aspects of practice organisation that affect them?
3. What are our most effective services for elderly people and what are the least effective? How could we improve our efficiency without adversely affecting the quality of care we offer? How can we evaluate the services we offer our elderly patients?
4. Could our practice have better links with our colleagues in other professions?

I think I have gone some way to meeting the challenge of this check list using the innovations described in the contribution.

REFERENCES

Almind, G. (1983) 'Medical care of the elderly in the community: The general practitioner's contribution'. Paper read at 31st International Congress of General Practice, Societas Internationales Medicine Generales, Klagenfurt, Austria, 23rd September

Barber, J. and Wallis, J. (1978). The benefits to an elderly population of continuing geriatric assessment', <u>Journal of the Royal College of General Practitioners</u>, <u>28</u>: 428-33

Elliott, A. and Stevenson, J. (1973) 'Geriatric care in general practice', Journal of the Royal College of General Practitioners, 23: 615-25

Freeman, G. Charlewood, J. and Dodds, P. (1978) 'Screening the aged in general practice', Journal of the Royal College of General Practitioners, 28: 421-5

Wilkinson, J., Stokoe, I. H., Gray, S., Fiser, M., Smith, A., McGhee, A. and Stephenson, E. (1964) 'Old people at home, their unreported needs', Lancet 1: 1117-20

APPENDIX A

December, 1982

Dear Patient,

We hope you are keeping well and it seems that this could be the case since it is some time since you consulted us!

If you have a problem regarding your health, we would be pleased to discuss this with you at a special session on Tuesday mornings from 10.30 a.m. to 12 noon.

At this session, the nurse, doctor and health visitor attend, and you will have a blood test.

The object of this clinic is to give health advice and to detect illness, which, is as yet, not causing problems.

We would suggest an appointment on Tuesday, ... at .... a.m.

If you cannot attend or would like an alternative appointment, please ring .... Please bring the enclosed form filled in when you come and also bring a urine sample. Would you go for a chest X-ray one week before the appointment please.

Yours sincerely,

L. A. Pike

APPENDIX B

Please attend for Medical Examination on Tuesday,
at 11.00 a.m.

Name .... Address ....
Date of Birth .... Occupation ....

1. Have you any particular health problem you would like to discuss at your visit? ....
2. Have you a problem such as pensions, allowances, housing, you would like to discuss with the health visitor at your visit? ....
3. Have you a persistent cough? ....
   If so, do you cough up phlegm? ....
   Have you noticed any blood in the phlegm?................
   Do you smoke, and if so, how many per day?...............
4. Are you short of breath on climbing the stairs?..........
   Have you swelling of the ankles?..........................
   Have you shortness of breath during the night?...........
5. Is there any family history of heart disease or high blood pressure?...
6. Are your bowels regular?.................................
   Do you pass blood with the motions?......................
7. Have you any pains or difficulty when you pass urine?...
   Can you control your urine flow satisfactorily?..........
8. Do you have headaches? (Please tick)
                    Regularly ....
                    Occasionally ....
                    Never ....
9. Do you take alcohol? (Please tick)
                    Regularly ....
                    Occasionally ....
                    Never ....
10. Do you sleep well at night? ....
11. Have you any hearing difficulties?......................
12. Do you consider yourself fit?...........................
    What is your height?...................................
    What is your weight?...................................
13. Can you (a) get about the house without difficulty?......
           (b) get out of the house to do shopping?.........
           (c) get away on holiday?.........................
Please bring a urine sample with you.

Chapter Five

EXTENDED ROLE OF THE HOME HELP SERVICE

S. Daffern

The past decade has presented local authority Social Services
Departments with many challenges, particularly concerning services to the elderly, such as the Home Help and Night Watch
Service. Social services departments are charged with a
statutory obligation to provide a home help service, but the
enabling legislation (1) does not specifically define the extent of a local authority's commitment towards the service.
The city of Birmingham, in setting up its service, chose to
interpret the mandatory legislation widely, offering the maximum rather than the minimum that the law required.

ORGANISATION OF THE HOME HELP SERVICE

The home help service receives referrals from social workers,
general practitioners, nurses, hospitals and rehabilitation
officers, as well as direct from clients and their relatives.
In addition to organising practical support, the service makes
its own referrals to specialist social workers, general practitioners, nurses and voluntary and statutory agencies on behalf of the client.
    The service in Birmingham is organised from 13 area
offices within four geographical districts. The areas vary in
size, serving from 430 to 2,000 clients each; and each is
managed by a team leader organiser assisted by assistant
organisers and clerical staff,with between 70 and 300 part-
and full-time home helps employed in each area.
    The role of the home help organiser is to arrange practi-
cal care and support to the client. In order to achieve that
aim the organiser's responsibilities include personnel management, planning,assessment of need and of financial resources,
and accountability as a public servant. The principal aims of
the service are:

    1.   To give practical caring support, by undertaking nor-
          mal household duties, to clients who are handicapped
          by infirmity or by acute illness.

2. To maintain clients in the community, thus preventing admission to long-stay residential accommodation and geriatric wards.
3. To achieve successful rehabilitation of clients discharged from hospital, in co-operation with other community-based services.
4. To ensure liaison with other voluntary and statutory agencies involved in the care of our clients.
5. To foster the motivation of clients towards self-help, where appropriate.

When I first became responsible for the management of the home help service in 1975 my first review suggested that a conventional home help service would be insufficient in the future to meet the needs of our clients. Imaginative and innovative schemes would have to be developed if the service was to remain a lynchpin of domiciliary care within the community. The problems which statutory services faced fell into four categories, demanding separate consideration.

1. There was a rapid growth in the number of persons aged 75 and over in the population. Table 5.1 shows population data for Birmingham Metropolitan District prepared by the Central Statistical Office of the local authority which confirmed this growth. To meet this growing demand, the DHSS document Priorities for the Health and Personal Social Services in England (1976) recommended the rapid development of NHS and social services domiciliary services by 6 per cent a year and the meals, home help and general social work services support by 2 per cent a year.
2. The increasing number of carers within the community who were coping with an ever-increasing number of stroke victims and patients with other physical and mental handicaps needed regular practical support to enable them to continue.
3. Many elderly patients who were being discharged from hospital into the community were unsupported because of breakdown in family structure, the children having moved away from the patients' neighbourhood.
4. Many old-established communities have changed vastly over the past two decades, causing many elderly people to find themselves isolated when their physical limitations result in their being increasingly housebound.

Table 5.1:   Population and Age Distribution 1971-1986
             Birmingham Metropolitan District

	1971		1976		1981		1986	
	Number	% Total pop.	Number	% Total pop.	Number	% Total pop.	Number	% Total pop.
65+	132,705	12.08	146,100	13.79	153,000	14.71	157,000	15.15
70+	82,330	7.50	93,600	8.84	101,500	9.75	106,000	10.29
75+	45,930	4.18	53,400	5.04	60,200	5.79	64,900	6.26

In order to develop the home help service to meet these needs
and problems, two financial strategies were open: the replacement of existing resources and the acquisition of new finance
from the Inner City Partnership and the Joint Funding Programme (2).

In the second year of joint funding,1977/78, many of the
proposals put forward were aimed at assisting old people under
the terms of DHSS Circular LAC (76)6. This group was intended
to benefit since half of the joint funding allocation was to
promote services for people aged 75 or over. In terms of joint
funding they were a particularly suitable group, since assisting in their care in the community would lessen the demand on
health authorities for geriatric beds.

SUMMARY OF INNOVATIVE SERVICES

Mobile home helps were first introduced by the department in
1977, to meet the urgent or special needs of clients through
a programme of short visits arranged daily. 1977 also saw the
introduction of a scheme providing for up to 15 hours' free
service to help clients who had been newly discharged from hospital. In 1978 one mobile home help was provided in each area
to cover weekends. In 1980 a laundry unit was established to
help with the needs of incontinent clients.

The night watch service, operational in Birmingham since
the 1950s, is organised from the central home help office. Increasing demand from very elderly clients led, in 1977, to the
acquisition of funds to support six additional night watch
posts for these clients, and a mobile night watch service was
subsequently established. From 1979, the home help service
has collaborated with the district nursing service, and,
latterly, with the mobile night watch, to provide a 'tuck-in'
service. The most recent innovation was the establishment in
1982 of five hospital-based home help organisers to initiate
the provision of practical support for people being discharged
from hospital.

Extended Role of the Home Help Service

MOBILE HOME HELP SERVICE

The first innovative scheme to take account of the increasing
number of people aged 75 and over living in the community was
the introduction in 1977 of the mobile home help service. Two
experienced home helps who had completed a training course and
were car drivers were appointed from the basic budget for each
of the 13 areas in the city, and were paid a casual car user's
rate, something not previously approved in this largely urban
authority.
    The staff reported every morning to their area office
where they were given a programme of visits to clients with
special needs,e.g.those who required urgent shopping, collection of pensions, or daily emptying of a commode; and those
who had recently been discharged from hospital, or who had
required any other essential service. It was expected that a
mobile home help would spend not more than 20-30 minutes with
each client. Their duties were viewed with some suspicion by
colleagues, but eventually they were seen to provide an important complementary service to that undertaken by home helps
working with clients long-term. The staff responded to the
challenge extremely well and within a short time home help
organisers were wondering how they had coped before the introduction of these staff.
    A review was carried out six months after the pilot scheme
commenced. The work pattern of the mobile home helps was monitored by the organisers and their opinions were sought about
the uses and benefits of the service. The greatest benefit was
the ability to offer to clients a reliable and immediate response to a request for help, particularly in emergencies.
    The mobile home helps were used most frequently for:

1. Clients needing early morning fires and breakfast.
2. Clients needing shopping.
3. Clients needing someone to 'pop in' during the
    regular home help's holiday or sick leave.
4. Clients discharged from hospital.
5. Clients considered to be living in an 'at risk'
    situation.

The organisers recommended expansion of the service and further
flexibility. A proposal was put forward for joint funding for
an additional 15 mobile home helps for clients recently discharged from hospital. This enabled us to ensure that help
was available for all patients discharged from hospital, about
whom we had been informed.

POST-HOSPITAL SCHEME

A problem in arranging domiciliary support for clients being
discharged from hospital was that, except for clients on

supplementary pension, a financial assessment was required.
Clients discharged from hospital to live alone often need help
during a 'settling-in' period. Some 90 per cent of clients of
this type are 75 years of age or more, and many refuse help
because they are not willing to be means-tested. As a consequence, they may return home to a cold unprepared house with
little or no food. A joint funded scheme was, therefore,
initiated to help this client group by offering 15 hours of
free service. In its first year of working, 1977, it was estimated that this scheme would lead to an annual loss of revenue
of approximately £12,000. During the earlier days of this
scheme the accounts procedure proved difficult to monitor;
while some new clients thought that all visits after the first
15 hours would be free. However, the arrangement was thought
to be successful even if a client refused help following the
15 free hours, since it is the first 48 hours at home after
discharge that are so crucial to a successful return into the
community.

WEEKEND SERVICE

Many domiciliary support services in the 1970s were still
offering only a Monday to Friday service. In Birmingham we
recognised that most people who needed five-day support often
needed help at weekends as well. The needs of those who lived
alone had been covered by staff who volunteered to work for a
few hours on Saturdays and Sundays but this could not continue
because the staff became tired and unable to offer the necessary level of care. It was, therefore, decided to recruit
staff who were keen to undertake personal care but whose
family commitments prevented them from working from Monday to
Friday. Four home helps were employed to work at weekends
only and to cover clients discharged from hospital just before
or during the weekend, particularly to give personal service
and provide food. The four members of staff, who were car
drivers, were expected to work for about five hours in the
morning and one hour in the evening. This scheme was such an
outstanding success that it was decided to fund out of our
growth budget, one mobile weekend home help in each of the 13
areas of the city.
    The high transport costs incurred by the four original
members were considerably reduced by the appointment of the
additional staff. The staff had to be caring and capable, as
no direct supervision was available; although senior officers
undertook to offer support and advice over the telephone.

LAUNDRY SERVICE

The health service had operated a laundry service for incontinent patients for many years but there was a lengthy waiting
period. Bearing in mind the fact that the Health Services and

Extended Role of the Home Help Service

Public Health Act 1968 stated that: 'Each Authority shall
have the power to provide or arrange for the provision of
laundry facilities for households for which home help is being
or can be provided' (Part I, Section 13.1), the department
proposed a small laundry unit which could be used by home
helps who were faced with heavily soiled, but unmarked,linen
in many houses where there were no suitable washing facilities,
particularly in inner-city areas. Normally, laundry was taken
to a launderette but this was not acceptable for doubly incontinent clients because the linen required extensive sluic-
ing prior to washing. A questionnaire sent to all home helps
confirmed the need for such a unit.
    A proposal was first put forward to joint funding in 1977
for four rooms in residential homes for the elderly to be converted into laundries, but this proposal was not accepted. In
1978 a request was made to the inner-city partnership programme for a laundry room attached to a small residential unit
in the inner-city. This scheme was accepted with a capital
budget of £22,000 and a revenue allocation of £1,400 each year
for three years. The equipment provided in the unit, which was
commissioned in September 1980, consisted of:

    Two fully automatic washing machines taking incontinent
        washing that had not been sluiced;
    an automatic system that fed detergent and bleach into
        the machines with many programmes of washing;
    one water extractor;
    two commercial tumble driers;
    sink and toilet facilities;
    irons and ironing boards.

When the laundry came into operation it was decided to offer
its use to the mobile home helps from four area offices situated near the laundry. The other nine area offices were made
aware that the facilities were available should they have a
problem with laundry that could not be solved in any other
way. Two training sessions were held for the staff who use
the laundry, and clear instruction leaflets were prepared
which have prevented any serious problems in the laundry's use
by staff who had not attended the training sessions.
    The problems encountered were:

1. The time taken to travel to the laundry unit;
2. The waiting period;
3. The mixture of fibres in one load with consequent
    damage to some of the washing;
4. There was occasionally over-demand on the launder-
    ette, particularly following weekends;
5. There were difficulties for home helps working with
    confused elderly clients, who had to explain why
    sometimes laundry was free and at other times they

had to pay when it was taken to a local launderette.

This unit has proved an extremely useful resource for the home help service. Further units have not been contemplated since the facilities meet the demand.

NIGHT WATCH SERVICE

The night watch service forms part of the home help/night watch service within the fieldwork division of the social services department. It is organised centrally to cover clients within the metropolitan district of Birmingham. It has existed as a domiciliary night care support service since the 1950s. The night watch service employs 80 staff, who provide help to 150 clients, on average, every month. Ninety per cent of these are aged 65 years and over.

The aim of the service is to provide night care to sick and elderly people in their own homes, either on a short-term basis whilst the patient awaits admission to hospital, or over an extended period when there is chronic illness or disability. In recent years the service has been increasingly involved in giving help to clients following long-term hospitalisation when the night watchers have been required to assess the ability of the clients to manage on their own during the night.

The majority of elderly clients prefer to spend their last days at home. This service enables us to meet their wishes, in many cases without excessive strain on the family. It also reduces the demand for beds in hospitals or residential accommodation.

The criteria for the services are that the client is unable to reach the commode unaided, or requires a considerable amount of attention during the night. Twenty-five per cent of clients suffer from terminal cancer, and close liaison with hospices and nursing services (see Chapter 14) enables us to offer very effective care to these clients and their carers. Additionally, help is given to relatives caring for physically or mentally handicapped family members of all ages who receive regular help, generally on two nights per week.

The service has never had a waiting list and aims never to refuse help where appropriate. In an emergency, help can be withdrawn from a case of lower priority. The needs of a person living alone are greater than when there are other family members present. On the other hand, we are sometimes able to give family cases additional support when another client no longer requires assistance.

The night watcher is expected to perform any task normally undertaken by a relative or friend. Applicants for night watcher posts are not expected to have a nursing qualification, although work in hospital as an auxiliary or as a care assistant in homes for the elderly has proved to be the most useful relevant experience.

Because of the increasing demand for help for clients discharged from hospital, an application was made in 1977 for joint funding for six additional night watcher posts and a further six posts were funded by the inner city partnership programme in 1978. This enabled us to cope with very elderly clients living alone, often within isolated pockets in the community and requiring considerable practical assistance during the night. Terminal and severely handicapped clients are given almost the amount of service which they have been judged to need, without reducing staff time for the most urgent cases. Training for night watchers has paid particular attention to the problems faced by staff working in comparative isolation, often with a degree of emotional trauma.

It became increasingly difficult for the four district managers, each already responsible for domiciliary care services in a quarter of the city, to continue management of the night watch service as a side line, particularly bearing in mind the rapid turnover of clients, and the need for clients to be visited and helped. In 1981 joint funding enabled us to appoint two night watch organisers. By means of a telephone link, these are now able to give support to staff during the night. Night watch organisers have also been able, after training, to offer pre- and post-bereavement counselling and advice to families caring for sick people at home.

Payment for this service presents problems because of the difficulty of assessing relatives financially at a time of distress. In November 1982 the social services committee agreed that the service would be free for the first six weeks, after which a financial assessment would be required, except for clients in receipt of supplementary benefit. This procedure will overcome the difficulties of collecting payment in short-term terminal cases. Where long-term help is required, Attendance Allowance, which was introduced by the National Insurance Act 1970, is generally payable. As its name suggests, this is an allowance related to the need for attendance rather than the degree of disablement. Attendance allowance is a tax-free benefit payable when someone is severely disabled and satisfies certain medical requirements concerning the need for attendance. After six weeks the client and relatives usually have the means to pay for the continuation of the service.

MOBILE NIGHT WATCH AND 'TUCK-IN' SERVICE

A further joint funded project was the appointment of two mobile night watchers with car allowances to cover the needs of clients on a seven-day basis. Although there are two posts, only one person is on duty at a time. Unlike the normal night watcher who is generally restricted to one client per night, travelling to work by bus (since they are classed as manual staff and are not eligible for car allowances), the mobile night watchers can visit two or more terminally ill or severely handicapped clients in their homes three times each night between the normal night watch hours of 9.00 pm and 7.00 am. The mobile night watcher's cars are linked to a commercial telephone-to-car service where messages can be left by, for example, the all-night emergency team of social workers. Night watchers can also be linked by ordinary telephone to police stations and medical services, and by radio to an emergency call sign with the police, because of opposition to staff working alone in the city due to fear of violence.

This service proved unpopular with clients, particularly when an all-night service had previously been provided. Some problems were: disturbance caused by barking dogs, neighbours becoming worried about comings and goings, and anxious clients unsure of the exact times of arrival of the night watcher. It was, therefore, decided after nine months to transfer these staff to the 'tuck-in' service,i.e.to tuck-in a client, ensure that medication has been taken, that the client had a hot drink and was in bed, and to secure the house before moving on. In this way, the mobile night watcher was able to help at least three or four clients before returning at around midnight to a family case where their late arrival was still helpful to the carer. This has been an outstandingly successful project and we have recently given up one of our night watch posts so that the money saved could provide additional car allowances for three more mobile night watchers.

When district nurses are involved with a client, 'tuck-in' services have been introduced using nursing auxiliaries. Close liaison between social services and the nursing service, has enabled us to work together. Night watchers assisted where there was no need for nursing but rather for a tending type of support. Many home helps also undertake 'tuck-ins' in liaison with the nursing services, so that we are usually able to offer a seven-night service over a short period. We should, however, require increased staff and car allowances to expand this service.

HOSPITAL-BASED ORGANISERS

One of the earliest projects, Home Help Organiser (hospital-based), undertook to ensure adequate planned domiciliary support for clients being discharged from hospital. Because of the need to justify to the Personnel Committee an increase in the establishment of staff in the section, it was decided to undertake a pilot study using some experienced organisers whose own case-loads were not up to the maximum. The main aims were:

1. To provide more satisfactory cover for patients on transfer from hospital to their homes;
2. to speed the provision of domiciliary support;
3. to increase awareness of the domiciliary services.

Extended Role of the Home Help Service

The project was part of an expanding programme of domiciliary
support. It set out to improve referral, assessment and follow-
up procedures and to develop closer links with medical, nursing and social work staff. As well as the individual personal
help given by the organiser to clients seen in hospital, the
officers set up good communication links and spread information on the domiciliary support services in Birmingham, including the other joint funded schemes: the mobiles, the 15-hours
free help, and the night watch service, which have been previously described.

The feasibility of this service was proved. The medical
staff and the social work team appreciated the scheme, and
benefited from the direct contact with home help organisers.
There were fewer complaints about difficulties of the discharge
of elderly patients. As the pilot project made use of existing
staff, its funding came within the budget allocation for the
service. Any extension of the project would need support from
outside the department.

A scheme was submitted in 1978 for five full-time organisers to work from hospitals in each of the five health districts of Birmingham. This was held up at the social services
committee due to a general freeze on the expansion of staff
numbers. At the time the proposal was turned down for joint
funding, although this decision was reversed in 1979. In the
event, it was not until 1982 that agreement for the establishment of these posts was given and the first organisers were
appointed to commence work in October 1982. It is envisaged
that each organiser will be responsible for requests for domiciliary support from all the hospitals within a health
district.

As well as the improvement in the services to those being
discharged from hospital, the introduction of these posts also
achieved more effective liaison between hospitals and domiciliary services in that the organisers had detailed knowledge
of the services available and the authority to commit resources.
There was also a more economic use of the organisers' time in
that fewer home help staff had to attend hospital case conferences which always entailed considerable travelling time.
These posts will improve the delivery of services in areas in
which, due to pressure on staff, hospital social workers were
unable to devote adequate time and attention to the preparation
of patients for discharge.

Hospital-based organisers will offer specialised assessment of elderly frail patients who are faced with early discharge from hospital who are in need of extensive domiciliary
care in the initial stages. Organisers will, in some cases,
take prime responsibility for clients where no other social
worker is involved.

CONCLUSION

I have sought to demonstrate how innovative services have responded to the needs of handicapped and elderly people who
require support in their own homes. It is not easy to offer
objective conclusions. However, there are some indications of
the success of the service. In every area office can be
found a file of letters of thanks. One of the letters is long
and beautifully written in the copper-plate hand of an elderly
daughter who had been supported in caring for her 98 year-old
mother at home until her death, thereby fulfilling her deepest
wish. Another is a small scrap of paper with just two words
written with a trembling hand. These letters and all the
others bear witness to the appreciation of the service of so
many clients and their families.

There is other evidence of the esteem in which the service is held by statutory and voluntary organisations with
whom we collaborate. Finally, we must note the high standard
of the staff, which contributes to the quality of service received by the clients. There is a low staff turnover of both
home helps and organisers. Their supporting work gives them
job satisfaction. They respond enthusiastically to training
opportunities and are motivated towards making a positive
contribution to the service.

In developing any future pattern of domiciliary care,
policy-makers should be guided by a philosophy where every
client is treated individually. They must, therefore, move
towards providing a service to the elderly which suits local
needs, yet is based on community patterns. Good liaison with
other agencies helps our elderly clients to achieve maximum
self care.

In the future, the number of home helps must continue to
increase on both demographic and social grounds. Only in this
way can society offer a real alternative to local authority
residential accommodation or long-term hospital care for those
people who require daily or more intensive assistance.

Statutory services are only one link in the chain of
community care for the elderly which includes families, neighbours and friends. I am confident that staff will continue to
be sensitively aware of future needs and will provide an answer
to the changing problems they face by the creation of yet more
innovative schemes.

POSTSCRIPT

There are many examples of innovation in home help services in
this country: Ferlie (1983) lists more than 30 in England and
Wales. Some innovative schemes provide intensive home care to
elderly clients with a view to obviating or postponing the need
for residential or hospital care, for example Coventry (Latto,
1980) and Barnet. Coventry and North Buckinghamshire provide

intensive home care for confused elderly people. In Bradford home care aides help clients outside normal office hours, including at weekends and sometimes at night. East Sussex provides a free post-hospital discharge service for two weeks, as also does Gloucester. The latter employs a hospital-based organiser. Many schemes use monies from joint funding or inner city partnership. A powerful impetus to service development is provided by the facts of demography; continuing emphasis on the desirability and economy of community rather than institutional care; and policy statements about affording priority to work with traditionally disadvantaged client groups including frail elderly people. The current economic and political climate favours emphasis on domiciliary care by low-paid workers. Thus the processes and outcomes of these service developments will be watched with interest.

NOTES

1. National Health Services Act, 1977, Schedule 8.3(1) and (2).
2. See Chapter Two, p.14 for an explanation of Joint Funding and Inner City Partnership programmes.

The views expressed in this chapter are those of the author, and do not necessarily represent the official views of the social services department of the City of Birmingham.

REFERENCES

DHSS (1976) Priorities for the Health and Personal Social Services in England and Wales, HMSO, London
Ferlie, E. (1983) Sourcebook of initiatives in the community care of the elderly,Personal Social Services Research Unit, University of Kent, Canterbury
Latto, S. (1980) 'Help begins at home', Community Care, 312, 15-16; and 313, 20-21

Chapter Six

HIGH-RISE SHELTERED HOUSING

David J. Priestnall

INTRODUCTION

Birmingham, as a major Housing Authority, is faced with two
apparently unrelated problems. First, it has to accommodate
and support over the next few years considerable increases in
the elderly population of the city in a period of limited resources. Second, it has a legacy of high-rise housing which,
in its present form, is not as popular as traditional forms of
housing and which has become associated with particular management problems.

A unique scheme has brought the solution of both problems
together in one programme. This chapter describes how the idea
has evolved by analysing the principles of purpose-built
sheltered housing and adapting and applying them to the existing high-rise stock.

In common with other metropolitan districts in the country, Birmingham has an ageing population with a significant
and continuing growth in the very old. The recognition of
this has had two immediate local effects. First, is has focused attention on the resource implications of coping with an
absolute increase in the very sections of society who place
four times the demands on health and social services as do
persons of younger age groups. Second, it has reinforced the
realisation that the vast majority of the elderly will live
and die in their own homes in the community, and that institutional care must be regarded as a last resort.

The 1981 Census has demonstrated how far the process has
gone already. Of the total population in the city aged
65 years and over, only some 3.7 per cent are not in private
households but are in some form of institutional accommodation. Of the 49,500 aged 75 years and over who live in private households, 45 per cent live on their own, or with people of pensionable age (23 per cent). Therefore, two-thirds
of the very old do not have younger people immediately available to support them in their own household.

When projections are made for the increases in the very

50

old the picture becomes more acute. While the proportion of
the population aged 65-74 years will remain almost constant
during the 1980s, the population aged 75 years and over will
increase by 18 per cent in ten years, an absolute increase of
1,000 each year to a total of 63,000 and representing one in
fifteen of the population.

Table 6.1:   Increase in the Percentage of Elderly People in
               the Population of Birmingham

Age Group	1971	1981	1986 (projected)	1991 (projected)
65 years and over	12.1	14.5	15.1	15.3
75 years and over	4.2	5.3	6.0	6.3

Source: 1981 Census

In anticipation of these trends the city initiated in 1978 a
special review of housing for the elderly through a joint working party of the housing and social services committee. It recognised 'that in practical terms most elderly people will have
to maintain their own independent lives within the community
for as long as possible. We, therefore, consider that the provision of new Warden Service housing should have a very high
priority' (City of Birmingham, 1978: para. 3).

An analysis was undertaken of the city's waiting and transfer lists to estimate the future demand for warden service
sheltered housing. Allowing for the re-letting of vacancies
in the existing accommodation it was estimated that some 8,600
units would need to be provided over the ten year period. Even
if the new building rate of 350 units a year were to be maintained this would only produce some 5,500 units including re-
lets, leaving a shortfall of 1,600 units. At this stage the
full potential was realised of converting the existing stock to
sheltered housing.

SHELTERED HOUSING PRINCIPLES

The concept of warden service sheltered housing has borrowed
much from the almshouses of the nineteenth century. Today they
span anything from a group of bungalows with a nominated 'good
neighbour' through to very sheltered housing with a wide range
of facilities and resident staff, little different in most respects from a traditional residential home provided under Part
III of the 1948 National Assistance Act. Given this diversity,
what are the basic principles of sheltered housing?

In contrast to what 'shelter' has come to mean today, the
original term, according to Butler, Oldman and Greve (1983),

was introduced in a Ministry of Health Housing Manual (HMSO) in 1944 which talked about building special housing for the elderly on sites 'sheltered' from severe climatic conditions. However, it is not by accident that a whole range of physical and emotional characteristics have now been attributed to sheltered housing by both providers and residents, and these vary in scale and intensity from scheme to scheme.

Security is an important element with design emphasising a grouping of units which together with a warden and alarm system reduce the feeling of vulnerability, particularly in an emergency. The dwellings are small and convenient with, in some cases, accessibility for wheelchair use. Social and community life is encouraged through the provision of a communal lounge and other facilities (eg laundry, guest room). At the very heart of the sheltered housing philosophy is the retention of the individual identity of elderly people by their status as tenants, having their own furniture, their own front door, paying their rent and being responsible for meeting the normal costs of running a home.

A distinction is drawn between care and watchful oversight on the part of the warden. If care is required (eg home help, nursing) then this is provided on an individually assessed basis, with the level of support being increased or decreased as required. The warden's role is limited to ensuring that the right services have become involved. Warden service sheltered housing, therefore, seeks to provide, by grouping elderly people together, the best of two worlds. First, it helps those who have certain limitations through age to enjoy social contacts and mutual support with similar people in a secure environment. Second, as the basic minimum staff input is restricted it does not prevent or reduce independent action and motivation on the part of the individual.

An analysis of these principles made it apparent that they are not dependent on the construction of new accommodation or on the selection of a special kind of elderly person. Existing small concentrations of elderly people can benefit in exactly the same way if a similar approach is adopted in their own accommodation to the provision of basic facilities and the appointment of a warden. This point having been successfully proved in converting low-rise flats and bungalows, consideration was turned to the potential of high-rise blocks.

EARLY HIGH-RISE INITIATIVES

Birmingham has the doubtful distinction of having within its ownership and management the largest stock of high-rise flats of any single authority in this country and possibly in Western Europe. Because of the post-war re-development programme during which some 60,000 high-density Victorian homes were demolished, the most urgent need was for modern replacement housing within the cleared areas, and since only some

40 per cent of dwellings could be built there, in outer
suburban locations as well.

These two complementary building programmes achieved
record-breaking numbers. In one year alone some 5,000 dwellings were built by the city. But to produce this quantity
required both non-traditional forms of housing (high-rise
flats, walk-up flats and maisonettes) and system-built forms
of construction. The former have left social consequences
and management implications which are still being tackled;
and the latter have left a potential legacy of fundamental
maintenance problems which are nowhere near being fully
assessed. It must not be forgotten that Birmingham was acting in a similar way to most other housing authorities faced
with such numerical shortages of good housing, and in line
with Central Government policy which gave direct incentives to
high-rise building through the generous subsidy systems. The
first high-rise block was built in 1953 and the last in 1972.
During that period 429 blocks above six storeys high were
constructed, amounting to 22,184 flats. This is equivalent to
a town the size of Hereford.

Most of the social research in the 1960s which was critical of high-rise flats concentrated on the potential damage to
the development of young children. However, the isolation and
restriction on informal social contact associated with multi-
storey living has a similar effect on the elderly. In an attempt to compensate for this, research was undertaken in 1971
in the social development division of the housing department
to find whether there was any way of linking elderly people
together and promoting social activities.

<u>Internal Telephones</u>
The first result was an experimental internal telephone system installed in Salisbury Tower, Ladywood. Based on an ordinary telephone handset system contained within the block it
linked elderly households together and with the caretaker who
acted as a 'good neighbour' in times of emergency. The direct
benefits of being able to call up and chat to friends and
neighbours - at no cost - were of greater value than the security aspect, and contributed to social interaction.

Unfortunately, although the system was evaluated (Hastie,
1974) and extended to a further eleven blocks, the Post Office
ruled that it contravened their monopoly over intercommunica-
tion·between separate dwelling units and that the system would
have to be licensed. The effective result of the licence was
to specify a system and equipment which conformed with that
installed for a normal telephone subscriber at an equivalent
rental! The existing systems were allowed to continue until
the equipment became too expensive to maintain and no further
expansion took place.

Community Flats

The provision of purpose-built tenants' halls had been a feature of the development of large Council estates of over 1,000
dwellings from the mid-1950s. The possibility of providing
much smaller facilities, particularly for high-rise blocks, was
investigated and the first community flat was opened in 1972
at Cambridge Tower, Ladywood. Since then eleven flats have
been provided by converting existing residential flats or under-
utilised storage space at the foot of blocks.

Although community flats were not intended exclusively for
the elderly, some have become used predominantly by elderly
people in the block. Through a management committee of residents these elderly people organise informal social activities
– for example bingo, whist drives and coffee mornings. They
also pay a rental and meet their running expenses for heating.

Door Entry Systems

Most of the management problems associated with high-rise
blocks relate to unauthorised access. Acts of vandalism, graf-
fiti, misuse of lifts and communal areas can be reduced if
greater control is exercised over who enters the blocks. The
first door entry system was installed in 1977 which allowed
residents to let in only those people given permission by a
particular resident. A series of buttons outside the front
door is used to call a particular flat. The tenant of that
flat can speak to the caller, verify that his call is justified
and activate a remote control release mechanism for the front
door. Again, the peace of mind given to elderly residents has
been particularly significant and a high priority has been
given to this programme. All 429 blocks in the city now have
this system installed.

HIGH-RISE CONVERSION PROGRAMME

Taken separately these various initiatives have made a significant improvement to the quality of life enjoyed by residents
of high-rise blocks, in particular the elderly. But taken together in specific blocks the similarity with the facilities
needed to meet the sheltered housing principles previously
outlined is only too obvious. Consequently, the transition
to incorporating all these facilities within specially selected
blocks where there were concentrations of elderly people was
made in 1978, with the conversion of two blocks in the Kings
Heath area of the city.

Pilot Project

In order to test the feasibility of converting blocks to full
warden service sheltered housing, it was considered important
to select blocks which were not only of the right size and in
the right location, but which had not suffered serious

management problems. The prime objective was not to demonstrate what could be done with 'difficult to let' or unpopular
blocks, but to investigate what alterations are involved, what
the reactions of existing tenants would be and the potential
of attracting other elderly people who needed sheltered housing to move to the blocks.

Brandwood House and Cocksmore House seemed to be ideal
choices. They were of the right size, located on a single
flat site close to bus services and were within walking distance of the full range of shops in the local High Street.
Built in 1964, they comprised 34 one-bedroomed and 33 two-
bedroomed flats, sufficient to justify one warden each in
addition to the shared resident caretaker.

The location was also ideal because of the potential demand. There were few other purpose-built sheltered housing
schemes either existing or planned in the area. But there
were council estates nearby with family houses which were
under-occupied by elderly people who would not leave the area
to transfer to smaller more convenient accommodation, but who
might be attracted to move to the facilities of sheltered
housing.

Following the decision of the housing committee in
September 1977, two major items of construction work were
undertaken which together cost approximately £700 per flat.
First, a large communal lounge, kitchen, office and toilets
was created by converting the ground floor of an under-used
two-storey car park situated between the two blocks. Second,
a large amount of work was undertaken within the flats because
of their age, to bring them up to current fire regulation
standards. One drawback was the absence of an alternative
lift serving each block. However, special arrangements were
made to ensure that lift maintenance calls would be responded
to urgently.

The initial survey of the blocks revealed 43 elderly
tenants, who were interviewed about the conversion. The only
concern and limited opposition to the proposals came from the
few young or middle-aged tenants who felt that they might be
placed under pressure to move out. Once they were reassured
that they could stay as long as they wished, and that they
would enjoy certain of the benefits themselves, the opposition
ceased.

For the elderly residents, however, there were significant gains and no increase in their rents! They stood to gain
a speech alarm system linked to the warden who would make
regular calls on them, a door entry system and controlled access
to the blocks, the communal lounge, and future lettings only
to elderly people like themselves. In addition, the provision
of a warden would enable them all to enjoy concessionary TV
licences.

The wardens, who provided relief cover for one another,
were appointed in October 1979, and January 1980. Although a

few of the younger residents moved out others decided to stay.
A later evaluation of the conversion showed that of the vacancies that had arisen, some were allocated to elderly people
moving out of family housing. The majority of the tenants
were delighted with the improvements made and the benefits of
having a residential warden. The cost of the conversion was
only a fraction of the cost of a 'new build' scheme which then
cost in the order of £13,500 per unit. It must be remembered,
however, that no extra units of accommodation were provided
and the net gain only arose when re-lets occurred.

Criteria for Selection
Once the success of the first two blocks had been fully evaluated, attention was given to preparing a programme for future
conversions. A further three blocks were quickly identified,
partly because of representations made by the residents themselves. It was apparent, however, that a much more systematic process would need to be devised to select from the
remaining 424 blocks in the city.
On the 15th July 1982 a report was submitted to the
housing committee seeking approval to the following physical
criteria for block selection:

1. Size   - under 70 flats per block;
2. Location   - access to shops, Post Office, chemist,
                 bus routes;
3. Gradient   - flat sites with no major change of
                 levels to facilities.

Some 322 blocks were regarded on these criteria alone as being
unsuitable for conversion. A second group of criteria, based
on social factors, were then applied to the remaining 102
blocks:

1. Elderly proportion - at least half the residents to
                         be of pensionable age;
2. Stability   - blocks with low turnover rates;
3. Local involvement - contact between residents and
                         outside groups.

Current Programme
In addition to the five blocks which had been completed, or on
which work had substantially commenced by April 1982, a further
twelve blocks were agreed by the housing committee in June
1982, and a further eleven blocks in September 1982. Expenditure for the programme was found in the Housing Investment
Programme capital allocation.
The door entry systems were included on a separate programme for the whole city, but the speech alarm systems were
installed in all 23 blocks by April 1983, and where appropriate
were extended to surrounding low-rise accommodation. The

communal facilities varied according to the potential of each
block. In some cases existing flats were reserved for conversion; in others, purpose-built common rooms are being constructed where land is available. Flats have also been reserved for the wardens. The final improvements are redecora-
tion of communal lobbies and areas, together with carpeting.
    The wardens are being appointed as each conversion scheme
is substantially completed. Until 1982 the speech alarm systems were monitored when the wardens were off duty by relief
wardens. However, great difficulties were encountered in recruiting suitable staff and schemes were either left without
proper cover or undue pressure was exerted on the full-time
wardens to give cover even when they were off duty. As relief
wardens had to have good access to the residents and alarm
systems they had to be resident on site, and this sterilised
a dwelling which could have been used by an elderly person.
    A major electronic advance in telecommunications enabled
all schemes in the city to be linked via the telephone network
to a central control, manned 24 hours to provide relief cover.
Undoubtedly, the revenue savings on manpower (the difference
between 70 relief wardens and five central controllers) helped
to justify the capital expenditure on the central control
equipment and the cost of conversion of existing speech alarm
installations to make them compatible with the new system.
Also it released sheltered housing for use by the elderly.
However, the potential of central control is of even greater
significance to the savings made and the more uniform level of
cover provided. The number of schemes can be doubled without
any major expansion of the equipment or controllers. Further,
any isolated elderly people in the city can be linked into the
system provided that they have a telephone line. The existence of this system has enabled high-rise blocks which have
been converted to sheltered housing to be monitored by central
control immediately prior to the appointment of a warden. As
the response to an emergency call has to be channelled through
a neighbour or friend nominated by the elderly person, this is
clearly no substitute for a full-time resident warden.
    Because Salisbury Tower had received both internal tele-
phones and a community flat, it was considered by the housing
committee that in spite of its size (116 flats) 65 flats
should still be converted to warden service with two resident
wardens. It will be necessary to monitor the success of
combining more than one warden within a block before embarking
on any further conversion of large blocks.

EVALUATION OF THE PROGRAMME

Although it has not yet been possible to undertake a systematic evaluation of the conversion of high-rise blocks to sheltered housing, there is enough evidence to demonstrate that
it has in general proved very successful and there is a high

demand for vacancies.

Interviews with residents have drawn attention to in-
direct benefits of the conversion. One lady claimed that she
lived for years in the same block as an old friend and neighbour from the area from which she was rehoused. But until
they met at a social event in the communal lounge neither was
aware of the other's existence.

One criterion of success is that the demand in the first
two pilot blocks from the existing residents is to move to
higher floors. There are also several examples of people who
have moved from large family houses and are delighted with
their flats and the extra facilities in the blocks. There are
no requests for transferring out and very few have left to go
to hospital or a residential home.

The conversion of 28 blocks will provide 1199 units,
which it is estimated will produce approximately 150 re-lets
each year. This is equivalent to building four new purpose-
built schemes each year. This programme thus contributes
significantly to relief of the shortage of accommodation for
elderly people.

With almost 100 blocks which could be tackled, the programme still has a long way to go. However, it is likely that
long before that number has been converted, it will be necessary to monitor the general acceptability of this form of
sheltered housing to ensure that, having overcome the immediate pressing shortfall, high-rise housing is still a realistic
and popular option for elderly people.

POSTSCRIPT

While there have been many attempts elsewhere in the country
to place restrictions on allocating flats in high-rise blocks
to young families with children, Birmingham was the first
authority to convert existing blocks to high-rise sheltered
housing. A review of various initiatives undertaken by housing authorities in the country in the use that they make of
tower blocks was published by the Institute of Housing in
Trends in High Places (Randall, 1983). The experience of
Birmingham is outlined with its pioneering two blocks in 1978,
but examples are also given of the Scottish Special Housing
Association in a sheltered housing conversion in Glasgow during 1982, and Solihull's conversion of Woodbrook House in
1981.

Birmingham has received considerable national interest
in the scale and extent of its high-rise sheltered housing
conversion programme, and following visits to the city, several
authorities are now considering similar projects including
Hastings, Southampton and also certain housing associations.

REFERENCES

Butler, A., Oldman, C. and Greve, J. (1983) Sheltered Housing for the Elderly - Policy, Practice and the Consumer, Allen & Unwin, London

City of Birmingham (1978) Report of the Joint Working Party of Housing and Social Services Committee regarding Housing for the Elderly, unpublished

Hastie, R. (1974) 'Phones for the elderly', Social Services Quarterly, Spring, pp.124-6

Randall, B. (ed.) (1983) Trends in High Places, Institute of Housing, London

Chapter Seven

DOMICILIARY PHYSIOTHERAPY FOR THE ELDERLY IN SOUTH BIRMINGHAM

Fred Frazer

BACKGROUND

The need for a domiciliary physiotherapy service for elderly
patients has been the subject of argument for many years. Although the first mobile physiotherapy service was started in
1949 and was registered under the Charities Act in 1960, there
was considerable resistance to such a development within the
National Health Service. Domiciliary physiotherapy was gaining acceptance in France, Australia, Canada, South Africa and
the United States of America between 1973 and 1975; but the
British attitude was influenced by the comment in the Tunbridge
Report (1972, p. 89, para. 301): 'We consider it to be an
uneconomical use of scarce skills for physiotherapists to give
treatment in patients' homes'.
    Physiotherapists have been attached to a small number of
general practices in London, Sheffield, Newcastle and Bourne-
mouth since the early seventies. In 1971 a Southampton physiotherapist undertook a six-month trial of physiotherapy,
concentrating on the treatment of children. This led to the
first NHS community physiotherapy service being started in 1973
where patients of all ages were treated outside hospital, including in their own homes (Compton, 1973).
    A working party was set up by the Chartered Society of
Physiotherapy in April 1973 to review the need for community
physiotherapy and to consider how such a service could be provided. An interim report in October of that year stated that
there was a great need for a non-hospital physiotherapy service. The McMillan Report (1973) provided additional support
for this view, stating: 'We welcome the involvement in the
community and see a greater scope there for physiotherapists
primarily in an advisory and preventive role'. (p.9)
    The remedial professions organised a joint working party
in 1974 which recommended that the DHSS should set up a project to consider the role of the therapist in the community.
A research physiotherapist was appointed in 1975, and a report
was published (Partridge and Warren, 1977) describing 14

60

Domiciliary Physiotherapy for the Elderly in South Birmingham

schemes providing physiotherapy in the community, stressing
the need for such a service.

The Need for Domiciliary Treatment
The advantages of domiciliary physiotherapy for the elderly
are:

1. Treatment in the home is seen as relevant by the
   physiotherapist, because problems within the home can
   rarely be effectively duplicated in the hospital
   physiotherapy department.
2. Problems may not even be recognised by the patient
   and, therefore, are not mentioned in a visit to the
   outpatient department.
3. The availability of support from family and friends
   can only be accurately assessed during home visits.
4. Any need for social services support can be assessed
   at the time of a home visit.
5. Many patients in the 65 and over age group are too
   frail to endure the strain of a journey to hospital
   for outpatient treatment. Even when a reliable
   ambulance service is available, the effect of treatment may be negated by the strain of the ambulance
   journey (Beer et al, 1974), and the waiting and
   travelling time.
6. Even when the patient is able to travel to hospital
   it is not always possible to ensure attendance when
   ambulance transport is required. Patients requiring
   two ambulance men to lift them into the ambulance are
   the first to suffer when there are staff shortages.
   During the period 1972-82, 18 per cent of all planned
   ambulance journeys to the physiotherapy department of
   Selly Oak Hospital, Birmingham, were cancelled without warning.

Disadvantages
The arguments advanced against a domiciliary physiotherapy service for the elderly are:

1. The physiotherapist spends a great deal of time travelling and treats only a limited number of patients.
2. Treatment is brief and infrequent and therefore doubt-
   fully effective.
3. Space is limited in the home.
4. Special equipment is not available.
5. Group treatment or treatment requiring two physiotherapists cannot be provided.
6. The scheme may attract staff away from the hospital
   department.
7. The costs are high.

61

SOUTH BIRMINGHAM DOMICILIARY PHYSIOTHERAPY SERVICE

A community physiotherapy service was established in South
Birmingham Health District in 1977. This service deals mainly
with patients aged 65 and over, although patients below this
age are treated at home if in acute need. The opportunity was
taken of analysing and costing its work, in comparison with
that of the conventional physiotherapy service to determine the
validity of the above arguments. The service will be described
here and some of the results of the analysis will be presented.

The Development of the Service

The need for a domiciliary physiotherapy service in South
Birmingham health district had been recognised for some years.
There was a successful attempt in 1974 to develop links with
the community when a GP direct access clinic was created
(Frazer, 1979a). This clinic operated each evening in the physiotherapy department at Selly Oak Hospital. GPs could refer
patients direct to the physiotherapy department, thus avoiding
the referral system via the consultant outpatient clinic. This
development ensured close links with the general practitioners
in the district so that when, later, a domiciliary physiotherapy
service was proposed it was relatively easy to obtain their
support.

In September 1976 meetings were organised with groups of
general practitioners. The GP representative on the Health
Care Planning Team for the Elderly was instrumental in dissemi-
nating information to his colleagues throughout the district.
The proposal was discussed by various planning, medical and administrative teams where the view was expressed that such a
service might deprive the hospital of physiotherapy staff. The
GP direct referral scheme had produced a similar reaction in
1974. Since that development had resulted in an increase in
applications from physiotherapists to work in the hospital, it
was pointed out that the domiciliary service might produce a
similar effect, as the department would be seen as innovative
and dynamic and thus attractive in terms of job satisfaction.

A pilot study commenced in March 1977 and preceded the
main development of the service. The study was based on eight
general practices in South Birmingham health district, and was
funded by redeploying an unfilled post from another hospital in
the district. The travelling expenses were provided by the
committee for locally organised research of the West Midlands
Regional Health Authority. Twelve patients were treated in the
pilot study, nine of whom improved. The major outcome of the
pilot study was a decision to allocate funds from Joint
Funding (1) to allow the employment of three physiotherapists
for domiciliary work.

Expansion of the Service

On the appointment of the three additional physiotherapy staff,

the service was publicised to the remainder of the 109 general
practitioners in the South Birmingham health district, by
letter, inviting participation; by meetings with the general
practitioner and district nurse community representatives and
with the community administrator; by a series of talks to
doctors, district nurses and other staff; and by the local
press, medical press and articles in professional journals.

The new domiciliary service provided an opportunity to
compare the cost-effectiveness of hospital-based physiotherapy
with domiciliary physiotherapy. A study was carried out during the period 1977-80 which sought to determine whether
treatment in the patient's home was as effective as treatment
in the hospital physiotherapy department and to determine
whether there was a difference in cost (Frazer, 1981). The
study affected the service to the extent that referral, assessment and outcome measures had to be clearly defined and
accurately measured.

Method of Referral

At the commencement of the service an open referral system was
used. That is, any professional workers involved with a
patient in the community could refer him to the physiotherapy
staff. The patient's general practitioner was informed of referrals from non-medical staff and invited to visit the patient. Of the first 600 patients referred to the service 334
(56 per cent) came from general practitioners; 173 (29 per
cent) from hospital consultants; 41 (7 per cent) from district
nurses and 18 (3 per cent) from geriatric health visitors.
Thirteen patients were referred to the scheme from physiotherapists in the hospital department; and the few remaining
cases came from social workers, occupational therapists and
other hospitals. Since these figures were compiled referrals
have come from local authority residential homes, private
nursing homes and stroke clubs.

General practitioners and hospital consultants recorded
on a referral card the patient's name, address, age, sex, diagnosis, medical history and drug treatment. Other referrals
came by letter, telephone or personal visit. The domiciliary
physiotherapist then visited the house, made an initial
assessment, and asked the general practitioner if he so
wished, to initiate a formal referral.

Criteria for Use of the Service

The following criteria were established for the research
project and remain in use:

1. All referrals were sent to the physiotherapy
    department at Selly Oak Hospital.
2. No clinical condition was excluded.
3. All referrals had to include a diagnosis and an
    assessment.

4. The initial treatment period was up to twelve weeks.
5. Treatment was given as often as was thought necessary by the physiotherapist.
6. Treatment was discontinued at the discretion of the physiotherapist.
7. An assessment was carried out by the physiotherapist on completion of treatment.

Assessment Methods

As the service was open to patients with any physical condition a system of assessment was devised which allowed a degree of flexibility. Three main elements were measured: function, pain, and the patient's satisfaction with treatment. The assessments used were simple and quick to complete while providing a fair guide to the patient's condition

Communication

A number of communication systems, both formal and informal, were developed. These contributed to the smooth running of the domiciliary service. Community physiotherapists attended the weekly geriatric team meeting where they met doctors, nurses, social workers, geriatric health visitors and occupational therapists for discussion of cases. Domiciliary physiotherapists also participated in community management teams. The community physiotherapy staff form part of the physiotherapy department of Selly Oak Hospital. They participate in on-call weekend duties and they maintain close contact with their professional colleagues, to refresh skills and to avoid the isolation that might otherwise affect them if they worked entirely single-handed in the community.

There is close liaison with GPs usually by telephone or personal visit. A feature of the domiciliary service has been the interest and help of the GPs. Each physiotherapist leaves her calling card and telephone number with her patients and they are free to contact her at any time. On occasions this can entail calls in the middle of the night and at weekends but the benefit far outweighs any inconvenience caused.

Treatment Procedures

Six categories of treatment were available within the community:

1. Advice and management instructions which were common to all treatments.
2. Exercise, massage, mobilisation, manipulation, postural drainage; none of which required equipment.
3. Heat treatment produced by apparatus including a heat lamp, hot water bottle and paraffin wax; and cold packs which in some cases meant a 1lb bag of frozen peas.
4. Ultrasonic, interferential therapy, low frequency

transcutaneous nerve stimulation and biofeedback requiring specialised electrical equipment.
5. Intermittent positive pressure breathing - confined
to chest conditions and using a portable respirator.
6. Traction - used mainly in cases of neck and back
pain.

The equipment required for the treatments was portable. The
domiciliary physiotherapy service also provides balls,springs,
pulleys, walking aids, sticks and crutches; goniometers,
peak-flow meters and dynamometers. The community administrator
provides bath and toilet aids, wheelchairs, seat lifts, hoists,
bed cradles, commodes, special chairs and beds. In an emergency the physiotherapy staff could also supplement the laundry
service for incontinent patients by providing disposable
sheets, pillow cases and incontinence pads. An ultrasound
machine was the most frequently used piece of equipment. The
remainder of the treatment procedures were used only in small
numbers of patients.
     The treatment facilities to the patient in the community
closely matched those available in the hospital physiotherapy
department. A few items such as electrical equipment, parallel
bars and lumbar traction facilities were available only in the
physiotherapy department, but in many cases the domiciliary
physiotherapist improvised by re-arranging furniture to assist
walking and by using skin traction to treat sciatica.
     There were specialised exercises for balance, walking,
moving around in, and transfer from, bed to chair or commode.
There were specific routines for patients with hip replacement
and amputation. The patient progressed through a carefully
controlled scheme of exercises. The patient and his relatives
were continually monitored during the course of treatment.
Patients were given a specially prepared exercise sheet detail-
ing their exercise and relatives were given advice and instruction on the supervision of the exercises. The presence of relatives during treatment was welcomed and the relatives enjoyed supervising exercise programmes (Frazer, 1981). Publications on stroke, or a specially written booklet were given
as appropriate to the patient. Three-quarters of the patients
treated had exercises only, demonstrating that an effective
domiciliary physiotherapy service for the elderly could be
provided with the minimum of equipment.

Duration of Treatment
Of the first 400 patients referred to the study, the number of
treatments given to elderly patients at home ranged from one
to 41, with a mode of twelve and a mean of seven (Frazer,
1981).   In consequence a course of up to twelve treatments is
given before a further assessment of the patient is requested.
Treatment is given daily initially, and reduced to once weekly
or as in the case of some old stroke patients, a visit once a

month is adequate to monitor progress and to provide advice and support to the relatives. On the other hand in some respiratory cases treatment has been given two or three times daily.

The age and sex distribution of the first 600 patients referred to the scheme and included in the study sample, is shown in Table 7.1. Although the scheme was intended for elderly patients, only 75 of the referrals (12.5 per cent) were under the age of 65. Otherwise the age distribution mirrored that of disability in the community. Twice as many women as men were referred; and more than one-quarter of all referrals were of women aged 75-84.

Table 7.1: Age and Sex of First 600 Referrals
August 1977- October 1979

Age Group	Men	Women	Total	%
0-64	32	43	75	12.5
65-74	87	119	206	34.5
75-84	63	175	238	39.5
85+	14	67	81	13.5
Total	196	404	600	100

The diagnosis is shown by age groups in Table 7.2. The diagnostic categories used were:

1. Stroke   – This referred either to fresh stroke illness treated ab initio at home; or to residual disability from an old cerebral vascular accident.
2. Arthritis   – This included both osteoarthritis and rheumatoid disease.
3. Fractures   – These were recent fractures of upper or lower limb.
4. Others   – These included a variety of neurological, cardiovascular and respiratory illnesses.

The distribution of diagnoses was similar in all age-groups. Stroke was the commonest presenting condition in men and arthritis in women, but the differences were small.

Table 7.2: Diagnosis by Age-Group in First 600 Referrals

Age Group	Stroke	Arthritis	Fractures	Other Conditions	Total
0-64	27	9	8	31	75
65-74	77	44	17	68	206
75+	89	103	47	80	319
Total	193	156	72	179	600
%	32	26	12	30	100

OUTCOME

Table 7.3 illustrates the outcome of treatment for the first 200 patients referred to the scheme and included in the study sample. They were treated between September 1978 and March 1979. In a group of 65 patients with CVA, 25 showed a favour-able response to treatment, 9 did not change (see Case Study A) and one was worse. The other 30 were lost to the study for reasons shown in Table 7.3. Even in patients who were assessed as not having changed there was often evidence that the morale of the relatives had improved. The advice and effort of the domiciliary physiotherapist alleviates many of the anxieties and worries felt by relatives nursing an extremely ill or dis-abled person at home (Frazer, 1981).

Case Study A
Mrs B was referred by her general practitioner with a dense right hemiplegia. She was five feet tall and weighed nearly twelve stones. Her husband who was six foot three inches tall and rather thin had recently been discharged from hospital having suffered a hernia while lifting her out of bed into a chair. They lived in an old detached house with narrow doors and dimly lit passages. Mrs B suffered considerable spasticity in her right arm and leg and was aphasic.

The domiciliary physiotherapist visited five times. She decided that any attempt at walking rehabilitation would be un-likely to succeed and concentrated on aspects of daily living to help the husband to cope with his wife. He and his wife were instructed in 'bridging' and 'rolling' and given the appropriate exercise instruction sheet. The physiotherapist organised a set of bed blocks which were made for her by the hospital occupational therapy technician. These blocks raised the bed by nine inches, converting a low divan into a bed which allowed the patient to rest her heels on the floor while her buttocks rested on the side of the bed.

On the third visit the husband was taught how to help his wife to stand up from the bedside and to sit down in her chair. On the same day her new wheelchair was delivered, her original

Table 7.3:   Outcome of Treatment - first 200 patients treated by diagnostic category

Diagnostic category	Remained on domiciliary physiotherapy				Other management			Died	Other*
	Much better	Slightly better	No change	Worse	Admitted to hospital	Transferred to day hospital	Transferred to Physio-therapy Department		
CVA	15	10	9	1	8	4	-	4	14
Arthritis OA and RA	8	19	7	1	8	1	1	-	5
Fractures	8	4	4	-	5	1	-	-	3
Other Conditions	10	19	13	-	7	3	2	2	4
Total	41	52	33	2	28	9	3	6	26

*Includes: 16 patients who did not require treatment; or who refused treatment; or who were unsuitable for treatment; or who preferred to have private treatment; or who had gone away.

wheelchair being too big to negotiate the doorways. She was discharged from treatment in August 1979. Her husband cried on the day of discharge, giving the physiotherapist a bottle of perfume as he was so grateful for the help he had received.

The couple are still living in the same house three years later, without any further physiotherapy help. This result at a total treatment cost of £30 is considered to be cost-effective and, although the patient's physical condition was not ameliorated, there was a significant improvement in her home life.

Case Study B

The patient, Mr J, was referred to the domiciliary physiotherapy service by his general practitioner, five days after Mr J's discharge from hospital. He was left-hemiplegic and his wife was expressing extreme anxiety at having him home. She was also upset as he was incontinent and she had to wash the bedclothes daily, by hand. She was unable to sleep because of worry about her husband's toilet needs.

Mr J was taught bridging and rolling on the first visit and his wife was given a supply of disposable urinals and incontinence pads. His wife telephoned the hospital physiotherapy department two days later to say that she was delighted, as she had had her first night's sleep since her husband came home from hospital. He was able to turn himself over in bed and to use his urinal when required because of instruction from the physiotherapist. In consequence the bed was now dry and considerable work had been saved. 'Advice and exercise' which is given routinely in the community, can considerably benefit patient and relative at negligible cost using simple procedures.

THE COST OF DOMICILIARY TREATMENT

The cost included salary, superannuation, uniform, travel, clerical, holidays and disposable items such as sticks, bandages and splints. In the sample studied the cost of travel amounted to 38 per cent of the total cost. The study took place during a particularly harsh winter when travel costs were high. The main cost to the physiotherapist was the purchase and running of a second family car. While running costs such as servicing, insurance and tax were covered by the regular user's allowance and the mileage allowance, paid monthly in arrears, this did not cover accidents, major replacements and depreciation. The nature of the work, which in a city involved frequent short journeys with starting and stopping, created a strain on the clutch and brakes.

The burden imposed by car purchase and maintenance might prove to be a disincentive to recruitment to the domiciliary physiotherapy service. There is also a non-monetary cost resulting from the physical and mental effort of dealing

with rush hour traffic, delays, parking problems, wrong addresses and the possibility in certain areas of the city of physical assault.

A Comparison of Domiciliary and Hospital Costs

There was little difference between the cost of physiotherapy
treatment given in the home and in the hospital department.
In 1979 the average cost for a domiciliary treatment was
£5.97 compared to an average cost of £6.93 for a hospital
treatment of patients matched for age and condition. When an
ambulance journey was included in a hospital treatment the
cost of each treatment visit to the physiotherapy department
rose to £14.97.

These figures correspond closely with the results of
studies carried out in Southampton (Compton, 1979), London
(Glossop and Smith, 1979) and Worcester (Moore, 1978). There
was a roughly similar incidence of improvement in the patients
treated in hospital and at home (Frazer, 1979b). As almost
80 per cent of the sample treated in the hospital physiotherapy department required an ambulance, it is clear that domiciliary physiotherapy treatment was the more cost-effective way
of providing treatment to elderly patients requiring transport.

PHYSIOTHERAPY STAFF

The constraint of car ownership influenced the selection of
staff. Part-time,mature, experienced staff were most suitable
for domiciliary work because single-handed working was lonely
and the work was often heavy. Staff employed in the South
Birmingham health district domiciliary service were encouraged
to develop another aspect of physiotherapy. One worked two
sessions in a group practice; one spent two mornings in the
physiotherapy outpatient department; one spent two mornings
on the wards at Selly Oak Hospital; while a fourth had a
session in the sports injuries clinic and a session treating
rheumatoid arthritis patients at Selly Oak Hospital. In this
way the strain of treating, single-handed, large numbers of
mainly heavily disabled elderly patients, was partly relieved.

The staff enjoyed the challenge of the work and were
heavily involved in medical, nursing, physiotherapy, occupational therapy and social work student teaching. They also
enjoyed an enhanced status as professional staff in the community. Their close relationship with their medical colleagues
encouraged the development of mutual trust and co-operation.

BENEFITS OF A DOMICILIARY PHYSIOTHERAPY SERVICE

At least half the patients referred for domiciliary physiotherapy demonstrated improvement following their treatment.
The criteria for improvement were the judgements made by the
patient himself; the GP; and a physiotherapist who had not

been involved in the treatment programme. Patients were described as 'much better' where all three judgements were of improvement; and 'no change' where only one or none of the three considered the patient to be improved. The results can be compared with a 'no treatment' group where only four out of 32 patients showed slight improvement following a three week period without treatment (Frazer, 1981). These figures suggest that domiciliary physiotherapy was effective. The results of treatment were equivalent to those obtained in the hospital physiotherapy department (with patients of that age group).

Many of the results reflected improvement in the quality of life of the patient or increased ability to cope with disability rather than dramatic improvement in the physical condition. In many instances the relative derived as much or more benefit from the intervention of the physiotherapist as did the patient, illustrated by Case Study B.

There were clearly savings on the ambulance service with consequential reductions in staff waiting time, wasted time caused by cancellation of ambulance, reduced burden on departmental, clerical and portering staff. General practitioners benefited from the presence of the service and some have stated that their visits to certain patients have been reduced.

The hospital doctor was able to discharge elderly patients in the knowledge that they would be supervised; this was particularly significant in older orthopaedic patients. The treatment was more relevant for the patient, his relatives, and the physiotherapy staff. Relatives' help was more readily obtained, treatment began sooner and the physiotherapy staff were able to act as a co-ordinator for several helping agencies. There has been a decrease of 14 per cent in ambulance patients attending the outpatient department for physiotherapy. During strikes which interfered with hospital admission and transport to the geriatric day hospital and the physiotherapy department, the true value of the domiciliary physiotherapy service was underlined, as patients were successfully treated in their own homes.

On occasions when relatives were reluctant to have a patient discharged from hospital, because of anxiety at having to cope with the work, the professional skills and specialised knowledge of the domiciliary physiotherapist provided reassurance and support. The domiciliary physiotherapy service supplemented the work of general practitioners, district nurses and social workers, enabling skilled treatment to be provided at minimum inconvenience to the patient, and improving communication and liaison between the hospital service and the community team. The ambulance service was relieved. Some patients were kept out of hospital; others were discharged earlier or with less likelihood of re-admission.

DISADVANTAGES

1. There are problems of finance, although a recently

announced government policy on 'community care' may
provide the means of improving this (DHSS, 1981).
2. There is a limit to the number of cases which can be
   treated each day, which involve heavy and demanding
   work, partly due to single-handed working, and
   partly due to the fact that travelling and administration accounts for approximately 30 per cent of
   the physiotherapist's time.
3. There is a limit to the type of treatment available
   (where bulky equipment is required) although this
   applies only in a minority of cases.
4. A major disadvantage is the requirement that staff
   are obliged to provide their own transport.
5. The service creates a demand which increases with
   rising expectations.

CONCLUSION

Domiciliary physiotherapy is now an accepted element within
South Birmingham health district, providing relief from pain
and expert rehabilitation to the patient in his own home, and
making full use of the potential of relatives to help. The
scheme is beneficial and effective. Similar schemes should be
established in other health districts.

POSTSCRIPT

The development of the domiciliary physiotherapy service, described in this chapter, has been mirrored by similar developments throughout the country. This increasing trend is reflected by the creation within the Chartered Society of Physiotherapy of a special interest group for physiotherapists working in the community.
    Three examples of similar developments covering the period
1976-79 in different parts of the country are mentioned below,
two from urban areas and one from a country district. Hampshire
Area Health Authority and Brent and Harrow Area Health Authority both offer domiciliary physiotherapy services within an urban
area. The Southampton service tends to concentrate on children
and young adults, but approximately 40 per cent of the patients
are 65 and over. The Northwich Park Hospital service has approximately 80 per cent of its domiciliary clients in the 65 and
over age group. These services have virtually identical average
treatment and travelling times with those of the South Birmingham service; and the average treatment costs of the three services are within a range of ± 20p. The Worcester service co-
vers a much wider geographical spread, and in consequence the
travelling time per patient averages 30 minutes per visit as
opposed to 15 minutes in the three other services. This time

Domiciliary Physiotherapy for the Elderly in South Birmingham

will be reduced when more staff are employed who can be based at specific points, thus reducing the distances involved. The predominant conditions treated in the three districts are broadly similar to those described in Table 7.3: namely, stroke and other neurological diseases, arthritis, respiratory and orthopaedic conditions. Similar benefits are reported and it would seem that a domiciliary physiotherapy service can be equally successful in either a country or an urban district. The increasing knowledge and information about such services will facilitate the setting up of similar services in the future.

NOTE

1. See Chapter Two, page 14 for an explanation of the Joint Funding Programme.

REFERENCES

Beer, T. C., Goldenberg, E., Smith, D. S.,Stuart Mason, A. (1974) Can I have an ambulance, Doctor? British Medical Journal, I : 226-8
Compton, A. (1973) 'The physiotherapist in the community', Physiotherapy,59,75-9
Compton, A. (1979) Personal communication
Department of Health and Social Security (1981) Care in the community, HMSO, London
Frazer, F. W. (1979a) 'GP direct access cuts waiting period for physiotherapy', Modern Medicine,April, pp.64-5
Frazer, F. W. (1979b) Evaluation of a domiciliary physio-therapy service to the elderly, unpublished M.Sc. Thesis, University of Aston, Birmingham
Frazer, F. W. (1981) Domiciliary physiotherapy: cost and benefit, unpublished Ph.D. Thesis, University of Aston, Birmingham
Glossop, E. S. and Smith, D. S. (1979) Domiciliary physio-therapy, Brent & Harrow Area Health Authority
McMillan, E. L. (1973) The remedial professions, DHSS Working Party Report, HMSO, London
Moore, A. M. (1978) Pilot scheme report for domiciliary physiotherapy, Worcester Health District
Tunbridge, R. (1972) Rehabilitation: Report of a sub-committee of the Standing Medical Advisory Committee, HMSO, London.

Chapter Eight

THE VOLUNTEER STROKE SCHEME

E. Staunton

BACKGROUND

The Volunteer Stroke Scheme (VSS) had its beginnings as long
ago as 1965. At this time the actress Patricia Neal had
suffered a massive series of strokes. Her husband, Roald
Dahl, understood his wife's urgent need for help and so he devised a plan for Patricia which eventually formed the basis
of the VSS. The plan was that a team of friends and neighbours would work with Patricia, at regular times throughout
the day, on all her many communication and speech problems.
One member of this team was Valerie Eaton Griffith, MBE, later
to become the organiser and driving force behind the VSS. As
time went by and Patricia began to show signs of recovery,
another patient, the writer Alan Moorehead, was introduced to
Valerie and the same methods were tried with him. This story
is to be found in 'A Stroke in the Family' (Eaton Griffith,
1975a). This is used as a reference book for the scheme.
Patricia Neal's much publicised recovery was followed by
hundreds of letters to her, her husband and Valerie from stroke
sufferers and their families all over the world. It became
clear to Valerie how great was the need to help stroke victims,
and so the idea was born of creating a national scheme, using
the same methods but on a wider scale and with the benefit
of professional advice.

The interest of the Chest, Heart and Stroke Association
(CHSA) was aroused and the Association sponsored two two-year
pilot schemes in High Wycombe and Oxford beginning in 1973.
The results were reported by Eaton Griffith (1975b). The
success of the pilot scheme led to requests for others to be
set up and, by April 1980, 33 schemes were in operation
throughout the United Kingdom, with more in preparation. In
1983 a comprehensive practical guide to working with dysphasic
stroke patients was published (Eaton Griffith, Oetliker and
Oswin, 1983). The South Birmingham Scheme was set up in
March 1980.

74

The Volunteer Stroke Scheme

THE SCHEME

The VSS was devised for people suffering from speech and communication problems as a result of strokes. Its purpose is to
encourage communication, however severe the loss of speech,
and to help overcome the resulting frustration, despair and
apathy. Difficulties with reading, writing, memory, concen-
tration, numbers, money and time are also given attention.
Above all the scheme seeks to increase confidence and to improve quality of life. It also aims to give help and support
to the patient's family. Volunteers, in teams of two and
three, go into each person's home on a regular weekly basis,
spending about one hour each with him. The patient is also
encouraged to attend a weekly club, run by the scheme supervisor, for which transport is provided. The volunteers aim to
stimulate the person through their own as well as the person's
interests and hobbies. A typical home visit might go as
follows: the first ten minutes or so is spent in talking,
finding out what the person has been doing since the volunteer's last visit, going over any homework which had been left
on the previous visit and chatting to the family. Then, if
for instance writing is a problem, help is given with written
exercises, doing a simple crossword or copying out a short
passage. The session finishes with something the patient enjoys, such as a game of cards or dominoes. It is important to
let the session finish on an 'up' note and to change the activity as soon as the person loses interest. Patients are encouraged to keep a diary or scrapbook which provides a talking
point and evidence of progress. As well, outings are arranged
to encourage a feeling of self-confidence and widen horizons,
which have been sadly narrowed, and to provide a talking point
long after the outing has passed.

ADMINISTRATION AND FINANCE

The CHSA is responsible for the VSS throughout the British
Isles. The VSS is administered from Headquarters at Great
Missenden, by the organiser, Valerie Eaton Griffith, and her
assistant, plus secretarial help. Each scheme is run by a
part-time paid supervisor under the direction of Valerie Eaton
Griffith. The average annual cost of a scheme with 26 patients
is £4,000 (at 1982 prices). This includes the salary of the
part-time supervisor and all transport and running expenses.
All work in the VSS other than the above is voluntary. It is
the policy of the CHSA to finance the first 15-24 months of
each scheme, and then to ask District Health Authorities to
'put up' the cost. Since 1978 most health authorities have
agreed to finance the scheme themselves after this period, provided it has been successfully established. Payment is then
made to CHSA which continues to be responsible for maintaining
the standards of the individual schemes. Each scheme is set

up within a health district or the equivalent, in which the
population varies from 100,000 to 500,000. It has been found
that a population of approximately 200,000 results in an average of 26 patients in a scheme at any one time.
    Requests to the CHSA to set up a scheme have come from
consultants, speech therapists, and individuals who have
heard about it and realised the need in their own area. No
new scheme is set up until Valerie Eaton Griffith has met and
obtained full agreement from the health authority, and until
eventual funding by them has been discussed. Contact is
established with consultants and speech therapists and a supervisor is appointed. A report is submitted annually to the
district management team on the progress of the scheme. This
procedure was accordingly followed in South Birmingham.

REFERRAL OF PATIENTS

People are accepted into the scheme by the supervisor, on referral by a doctor; or by speech therapists, nurses or social
workers with the doctor's agreement. Not all those referred
are suitable for the VSS, and the supervisor has the final decision since she alone knows what the volunteers can manage.
In most cases once a patient is accepted, he stays with the
scheme for a year or more; but for certain patients such as
the very old or deaf, an initial trial period may be agreed.
People are free to leave the scheme at any point, though in
practice few do. The reasons for leaving include that the
person feels he can manage alone, and that he has improved
sufficiently to lead something like a normal life without the
help of his volunteers. When someone has 'finished' with the
scheme the supervisor maintains contact by inviting him to
outings and social functions at the club.
    In March 1983, the South Birmingham scheme was involved
with 28 stroke patients, ten women and 18 men. Eleven of these
suffered severe communication problems; 13 experienced quite
considerable problems and just four patients had only slight
communication problems. Eleven people had useless right
hands. Seventeen patients were 65 years old or more, ten were
between 45 and 64 years old, and one was less than 45 years
old. Thirteen patients had both attended the club and had
home visits; eleven just attended the club, and four just had
home visits.

THE ROLE OF THE SUPERVISOR

As supervisor, I have full responsibility for the day-to-day
running of the VSS. In the early stages of setting up the
scheme I spent time making contact with local hospitals and
all relevant medical and paramedical personnel, the social and
nursing services, existing stroke clubs and voluntary organisations. I sent letters to hospital consultants and general

practitioners, announcing that the scheme was ready to start.
As soon as a patient is referred, I visit his home to explain the scheme to him and his family. During this visit I
make detailed notes on any problems the person is experiencing,
his hobbies and interests, his former job, and any other information which may have an influence on recovery. These notes
form part of the records kept for each patient. I explain how
the scheme works, what sort of help is offered - volunteer and
club - and ask the person and his family if they would like to
take part. Depending on his needs, I then decide on a suitable
programme of work and select a team of volunteers. Contact is
maintained with the speech therapist and GP, from whom advice
and assessment is obtained whenever possible.
        Another important part of my job is the organisation and
running of the club, which most people will attend. I arrange
transport to and from the club and organise the activities,
bearing in mind the differing needs of the patients. As it is
important to keep the patients interested in the activities on
offer, the club's programme varies from week to week. A typical
session might go as follows. The first half of the session
might be spent on various table games, board games and card
games for small groups. A break for refreshment is followed by
an activity which includes all members of the club; for instance a question and answer game, team games, magnetic darts
or indoor bowls. One person is helped to keep the score for
his team. This is always a good time to encourage use of
people's unaffected hands, as it has been noted that many of
them are reluctant to use the left hand. It is often during
this informal relaxed period that speech seems to come more
easily to some. Whatever the activity, it is important to make
it as enjoyable as possible. The purpose of the club is two-
fold; to provide an environment within which people use language and gain confidence; and to encourage people to mix,
make new friends and enable them to draw courage from each
other. Creating a relaxed and friendly atmosphere is a vital
prerequisite to encouraging the use of language. Experience
has shown that question and answer games are among the most
successful in relation to the latter. Many visitors, including medical and paramedical personnel, come along to the club
to watch, join in, and learn all aspects of the scheme.

PROBLEMS WITH TRANSPORT

In the early 1980s, levels of unemployment and short-term working in the South Birmingham area reduced the number of people
with cars available for transporting patients on outings and to
and from the club. Transport therefore has been a major head-
ache in this area. We have been fortunate in obtaining the
services of an enterprising young man who has set up a thriv-
ing private ambulance service, which we use to pick up those
who live in the south of the area. We had been using an

ambulance provided by one of the statutory bodies, which was cheaper but was dogged by delays and restrictions which marred the smooth running of the enterprise. Cost apart, therefore, we now have the benefit of cheerful, reliable and, above all, caring drivers who get to know the people and play a not inconsiderable part in the weekly club outing.

THE VOLUNTEERS

The scheme would not function without the loyalty, help and hard work of the volunteers. Some schemes find it easier than others to recruit sufficient volunteers. It helps if the supervisor has a wide circle of friends to draw on in the beginning.

Methods of Recruitment

The VSS in South Birmingham has tried various methods of attracting volunteers. The CHSA print a poster setting out the aims and objectives of the VSS which can be displayed in public libraries, health centres, shop windows, etc. This is known as the 'Come and Join Us' poster, and is accompanied by small pamphlets with a tear-off strip giving the name and address of the supervisor. In addition advertisements are placed in newsagents' windows in the areas where volunteers are most needed. It is sometimes possible to recruit volunteers via the secretaries of local organisations, and one particularly successful way of reaching a larger audience is by way of a Public Service Announcement (PSA) on local television. Seasoned volunteers sometimes recruit their friends into the scheme. Not all potential volunteers are suitable; for instance, of over 60 people replying to a PSA only ten were eventually allocated to a patient. Some lived too far away, some had misunderstood the need and the work involved. There were those who clearly had insufficient time at their disposal to maintain a regular weekly pattern of help. All who contact me are interviewed, and the details and methods of work explained. It is made clear at this first meeting that in order that a close eye is kept on people's progress, regular contact with me as supervisor is an essential part of the work involved, as also is attending six-monthly meetings with the other members of the team, including, if possible, the speech therapist. As well as volunteers to work with people in their homes, a regular supply of reliable helpers is needed to help with the weekly club, and in some cases with their transport to and from the club. Some volunteers are happy to be involved with both aspects of the scheme. I try to arrange for each new volunteer to pay at least one visit to the club. This seems to be a good way of helping the volunteer to appreciate the many ways in which people are affected by their stroke. It is sometimes impossible to find sufficient volunteers in particular areas, in spite of local advertising, newspaper

The Volunteer Stroke Scheme

articles and the like. One way around this problem is to arrange for a small number of people, and one volunteer, to meet in one person's house, thus forming a 'mini-club'.

Of the 39 volunteers currently working within the scheme in South Birmingham, one is aged under 20 years, 19 are in the range 30-40 years, and the remainder are aged 40-70 plus. Of the 39, only four are men. About three-quarters have some form of occupation outside the home. Two volunteers have themselves suffered from stroke illness. Six volunteers visit more than one person, and three of the regular helpers at the club also visit people in their homes.

Assigning the Volunteers

The volunteers are almost always strangers to the patient and his family. This is to the good, since they only know the person as he is now, and do not feel tempted, as so often happens with old friends and relatives, to compare him with his former self. They visit because they want to and not out of a sense of duty, their only motive being to help in any way they can, their only reward the friendship of the person and his family. As the volunteers see a great deal of the families, they are used as a sounding board for the family problems and come to be seen very much as family friends.

Where possible the volunteers are matched to the patients; for example, some people ask for a female volunteer only. Often patient and volunteer have a hobby in common; it makes life simpler for both parties if they have some starting point for future discussion. For example one person was having great difficulty in handling money and numbers. His volunteer 'followed the horses', so together they spent many happy hours placing imaginary bets and working out the winnings. Another person with severe dysphasia had been a keen gardener before her illness. She and her volunteer, another keen gardener, worked over a number of weeks on the garden. They used seed catalogues and planned a year's work with the aid of scrap-books and pictures cut from the catalogue. In this way people look forward to and contribute something of their own ideas to the weekly visits.

Most people have at least two volunteers who divide the problem areas between them, so that, for example, one works on numbers, time and calendar, and the other on memory, word-finding tasks and writing. Many volunteers encourage the patient to keep a diary. They are always surprised when they look back over the weeks and months, to see how they have progressed from the first tentative, wobbly words, to whole descriptive passages. One volunteer in the South Birmingham VSS kept a file on the person she was helping, which was of great value to the supervisor and the rest of the team. Each week's lesson was there for all to see and learn from.

When someone has been with the scheme for a length of time during which he has made good progress it is sometimes

better for him to be slowly weaned from the weekly visits, in
order to regain independence. One volunteer will be left to
keep a friendly eye on him, whilst the rest of the team go
on to help another sufferer.

Training and Support of Volunteers

One question often asked is what training is given to the volunteers. The answer is none. Each volunteer is given a
briefing on the person by the supervisor. A programme of work
is allotted to the team, bearing in mind the person's particular problems, and the relationship between the volunteers and
the individual determines the rate of progress. Suggestions
are put forward by the supervisor as to how the first few
visits might take shape. After that the volunteers are more
than willing to find their own solutions to problems. It has
been found useful in the early stages to keep in close touch
with the speech therapist and to arrange for the volunteer to
sit in on a speech therapy session.

It is important that the volunteer should not feel isolated in her work, since it is by its very nature a solitary
business. In order to keep the volunteers happy and feeling
part of a whole, the supervisor organises the occasional get-
together for all the volunteers, perhaps arranging for an interesting speaker to come along to answer questions relating
to the rehabilitation of stroke victims. This is also a good
time to swap ideas, voice worries and find out more about the
important work the volunteers are doing. If I were to be
asked what qualities make a 'good' volunteer, I would say, a
sense of humour; an ability to press on even when someone
seems to be making little or no progress for weeks on end;
and an enquiring mind.

Volunteers and Patients' Families

Much support is needed and given to the families of stroke
victims by the scheme. They are encouraged to take an interest in the work of the volunteers. They often contact the
supervisor for advice on the problems which afflict a family
with a disabled member. They are made welcome at the club and
are pleasantly surprised to see how well their relatives cope
with the many people, sufferers, visitors and helpers to be
found there. They pick up ideas and advice, from other wives
and husbands, by talking in the informal atmosphere of the
club. Some schemes have started relatives' groups who meet
elsewhere to offer support and companionship to each other.
This has not been necessary in South Birmingham, since a number of relatives got to know each other through meeting at the
hospital when the patients attended for speech therapy, and
a spontaneous 'group' was formed. Loneliness and isolation can
affect the families of stroke victims more deeply than is suspected by the general public. The effort of trying to cope
with what has happened to their loved ones can alter their

whole lifestyle. They often have had no previous experience of stroke illness and are at a loss as to how to carry on a normal life centred around the stroke victim. The volunteers help the relatives to keep a sense of proportion, by taking on some of the strain of finding ways of communicating with this stranger in their midst, this person, who looks like the one they have known, and loved, for so long; but who suddenly, without warning, is so different. The volunteer almost always becomes a friend of the family, someone who understands the strain they feel, the disappointments they have to contend with; someone in whom they feel able to confide their anger and frustration; above all someone they can rely on to turn up week in week out, not out of a sense of duty, or because it is their job, but simply because they want to; in short someone who cares.

PATIENTS' HISTORIES

The supervisor invites comments from the patient's GP, speech therapist and family after he has been with the scheme for about six to nine months. The histories which follow have been selected to illustrate different aspects of the problems. As the examples show, progress in overcoming communication difficulties is intimately linked with the characteristics of family relationships. The social context of communication problems are as central to the work of the VSS as are the communication problems themselves.

Victims often feel depressed and isolated. Case no.1 illustrates this. In many instances, families have different problems with which to come to terms. There may be family strain; and conflicts of interest between a patient and his spouse; case no.2 presents an example. Families may also need help to discover their own potential and unique contribution to the stroke victim's recovery of self-confidence, as case no.3 shows.

Depression and Isolation

Case No. 1. A woman of 74 joined the scheme five months after suffering her stroke. In hospital she was very confused and thought that there was no hope of ever being able to manage at home. She was tearful and worried that her husband, who was nearing his eighty-first birthday, would be unable to cope with her and the house, once she was discharged from hospital. When she joined the scheme her speech therapist suggested only one volunteer at first and no club attendance, since she feared that the woman would try to push herself too hard and become depressed at slow progress. The woman's children lived some distance away and she was anxious about their reaction to her inability to make herself understood and to hold a 'proper' conversation. She was reluctant to have them call to see her. During my first visit, she wept through sheer frustration at

not being able to answer quite simple, gentle questions as
fully as she wanted to. However, she was reassured that with
patience and the help of a volunteer things would soon seem
much better. From the first visit by her volunteer, the situation began to improve. They liked each other at first sight,
and she no longer felt so alone. Something which had been
worrying her a great deal was her inability to write. She had
kept a diary all her life and it was important to her to be
able to do so again. With encouragement from her volunteer
she soon learned to write with her left hand, and most days
was able to write a word or two. Her volunteer contacted her
family and asked them to call more often for short visits.
This cheered the woman and relieved the pressure on her elderly husband. After about five months she started to go to the
weekly club. She was quiet at first, but after a few weeks
she gained confidence and was soon joining in all the activities and looking forward to the club outings. As she gained
confidence in her ability to express her thoughts and feelings
on paper she became more adventurous in her use of spoken
language. Her volunteer encouraged her to carry out little
tasks around the home, such as dusting and washing up her own
cup and saucer. On one occasion her volunteer was presented
with a home made sponge cake she had baked. It had taken all
afternoon, but she had got there in the end and was proud and
happy. Eighteen months after first joining the scheme she is a
happy busy lady, who makes regular visits to her son and
daughter, and who is far more concerned with other people's
problems than with her own.

Conflict of Interest between Patient and Spouse
Case No. 2. A man aged 62 joined the scheme two years after
suffering his stroke. The man was bedridden following his
stroke. Some years previously his left leg had been amputated
following an accident, and as a result of the stroke his
right leg was useless. His wife talked non-stop during my
first visit, and did not allow her husband to answer any of
the questions I asked of him for himself. She seemed surprised
at the suggestion that he might be able to answer for himself,
given the chance! He did not look up once and seemed unaware
of a third person in the room. Two volunteers were found for
the man, who agreed to receive visits for an initial period
of one month. They found that he could say 'Yes' and 'No' and
that he was able to play a game of draughts quite successfully.
One of the volunteers encouraged him to write the odd word or
two, and with help he was able to complete a simple jig-saw.
Progress was painfully slow, mainly due to the man's wife, who
seemed incapable of leaving the room for more than a few sec-
onds at a time. She was very house-proud and reluctant to
have her routine upset. The volunteers agreed to carry on for
a few more weeks as they thought he was beginning to show more
interest in their visits. One of the volunteers had a young

son and daughter who occasionally came with her to visit. During one of her visits the man suddenly laughed out loud, for
the first time in weeks, and said 'Lovely children, lovely
children'. He was much brighter after the visits of the volunteers, but it was very difficult to persuade his wife to stop
treating him like a baby and to allow him to do things for
himself. One of the volunteers, a middle-aged man, suggested
taking him out in his wheel-chair for a short trip around the
local park. It took six weeks before the wife would allow her
routine to be disrupted in this way. Eventually the great day
arrived and off they went, to the great delight of both patient
and volunteer. They got lost and the volunteer had to ask the
man to direct him home again, which he was able to do without
any problem at all, relying on gestures and grunts and the odd
left and right. Sadly they were never again allowed to repeat
their adventure. The wife always found some excuse to put it
off into the future. Although the wife was always very lavish
in her praise of the scheme and the two volunteers, clearly
the only way she was able to cope with the situation was by
having a strict routine and sticking rigidly to it, refusing
all offers of help from outside sources, except on her terms,
to the detriment of her husband's possible recovery. The man
looked forward to the volunteers' visits, began to take an interest in television, and was much more alert for longer periods of time. If they achieved nothing else they were bringing a little of the outside world into his life. His health
deteriorated and the volunteers had to stop visiting for two
months during which time he slipped back to the withdrawn
state he had been in at the beginning. With a lot of patience
and tact it is hoped that the volunteers will be able to moti-
vate this man again and somehow help the wife to loosen the
'apron strings' for both their sakes.

Loss of Confidence
Case No. 3. A man aged 49 joined the scheme three years after
suffering his stroke. This man was referred to the scheme by
his GP as a 'last ditch' effort to help him. He lived at home
with his wife and two teenage daughters. Before his stroke he
had been a keen 'do-it-yourself' man, and worked at one of the
big car manufacturers in Birmingham as an engineer. The whole
family was quite devastated by the stroke. He had very little
speech, his comprehension was poor, he found great difficulty
in walking,and his right arm was virtually useless. Life as
they had known it had come to a dead stop. His wife was very
anxious about the future and was at a loss to know what to do
to help him. At my first visit I found a tearful wife and a
totally silent husband. He was clearly deeply embarrassed
by his condition and made no attempt to answer any of the
questions put to him. He indicated by a nod of his head in
the direction of his wife that she would be doing the talking
for him. He had had some speech therapy without much success,

but this had been discontinued because it clearly distressed him. They agreed to have one volunteer at first, also that he would attend the club for a few weeks. If he decided that he did not want to continue no pressure would be put on him to do so. He was very worried about his first visit to the club, but, surprisingly, he joined in with the activities straight away and seemed much more relaxed at the end of the first session. His volunteer worked with him on simple word recognition exercises, encouraging him to repeat the words after her. It took a long time and a lot of coaxing to make him say anything spontaneously, and he seemed afraid of making a mistake. He refused to go along on the first outing arranged after he joined the scheme, as he did not feel confident enough to cope with strangers. The volunteers found that he hardly walked anywhere other than in the house and on club days, out to the car and back again, so she decided to take him out for a short walk on each of her visits, increasing the distance by a few yards each time. He hated the thought of people looking at him. It had not occurred to his family to find out why he didn't walk. They assumed, wrongly as it turned out, that he could not manage more than half a dozen steps. Encouraged by the success of the volunteer's efforts, they now often take a ward around the nearby park. He gets the much needed change of scene and they are able to do things together as a family once more. Some twelve months after first joining the scheme the member is growing in confidence. He makes a big effort to say things and his sense of humour has returned. His wife has now returned to her job and is less anxious about the future.

APPRAISAL

One of the many problems which has come to light as the scheme has developed in the South Birmingham district has been the lack of information about, and consequent lack of understanding of, stroke illness and its outcome as far as sufferers and their families are concerned. On the whole very little information seems to be offered at the outset about the help which is available, whether in the form of aids in the home, or the availability of various kinds of therapy. It might be that the families are not asking the right questions of their GP or social workers, but whatever the reasons, the result is that the family is often left totally bewildered and at a complete loss as to how to cope with what is for them an immense problem. The victim has been discharged from hospital into their care, and many families have no real understanding of what to expect by way of subsequent recovery, and what steps to take to help in the process of rehabilitation. The people who are referred to the scheme are fortunate in that they are almost all having some speech therapy, but even this has to come to an end, and many of the problems of day-to-day living remain unresolved. The scheme succeeds in some of these problems by offering open-ended support to both member and family. As has been shown above, volunteers can often help, for example, by suggesting to the family ways in which the weekly routine could be altered to make more time available to spend with the sufferer. It often comes as a surprise to the family of a severely disabled individual, how lonely he feels when constantly sheltered from the everyday problems which arise in any home. The shame attached to stroke illness, the feeling that somehow someone is to blame for what has happened, is seen all too frequently. Sufferers are often isolated and lack any kind of outside social contact, especially in the mainly working class families from which most of the members in the South Birmingham scheme come. There has, on occasion, been a marked reluctance from the families to have more than a maximum of two volunteers visiting in the home. The value of conversation with someone who can contribute little more than 'Yes' and 'No' has been difficult to justify in some cases. As one wife pointed out, her husband had spent his entire working life on an assembly line offering him little opportunity to do much talking. When at home he had often been too tired to do more than settle down in front of the television, thus to start holding conversations now seemed pretty pointless and what were they supposed to talk about? Most of the volunteers come from a middle class background, are better educated than the people they visit and more used perhaps to asking questions and getting answers. Provided volunteers are able to overcome the initial barriers to establishing relationships, their attributes often enable them to assist in resolving the problems which the clients of the scheme may have found intractable. The fact that turnover among volunteers and members is low strongly suggests that the scheme is meeting a range of needs successfully. Although no formal evaluation of the South Birmingham scheme has been attempted, studies in other districts suggest that the general approach of VSS is successful in encouraging the victims' speech development (Meikle et al, 1979; Eaton Griffith and Miller, 1980).

As to the future, the scheme will continue to develop along the guidelines laid down by Valerie Eaton Griffith. The special characteristics of the area in which we work - the limited resources available to help stroke victims and their families and the class background of patients and volunteers - will continue to influence the way in which these guidelines are interpreted.

POSTSCRIPT

In 1983 the VSS covered one-quarter of the United Kingdom and to achieve that had taken nearly a decade. The idea of a similar service in every district still seems a long way away, and raises the questions of whether every district needs a

service and whether the present way of providing one is the
only way. Expansion is limited partly by shortage of funds
locally, which need not prove an insurmountable barrier, since
the sums required are small. A more fundamental limitation is
the natural desire of the CHSA to retain its control of the
scheme, especially by the selection, training and continuing
support of the local organisers, in order to ensure that volunteers of the right type are recruited, trained and retained.
As a relatively small charity, with many other calls on its resources, the CHSA cannot expand as rapidly as the demand requires. If it were to do so the service might lose the personal links between member, relative, volunteer, supervisor
and organiser on which the success of the whole system depends.

The CHSA's way is not the only one of bringing volunteers
to help in the re-socialisation of aphasic stroke victims.
There are other voluntary groups, such as Aid for the Dysphasic
Adult; while many speech therapists have organised their own
local groups of volunteers. But the current staffing levels
of speech therapy services limit the ability of the NHS to devote time to the recruitment and support of volunteers. In the
near future at least it therefore looks as though the rate of
expansion of the service will not greatly increase. However,
other countries have taken up the idea in different ways; and
Canada for example is making provision for the recruitment of
voluntary workers to aid dysphasic and other disabled adults
as a structured part of their health service provision.

REFERENCES

Eaton Griffith, V. (1975a) A Stroke in the Family, Wildwood,
London
Eaton Griffith, V. (1975b) 'Volunteer Scheme for Dysphasia and
Allied Problems in Stroke Patients', British Medical
Journal, September 13th, 633-5
Eaton Griffith, V. and Miller, C. (1980) 'Volunteer Stroke
Scheme for Dysphasic Patients with Stroke', British
Medical Journal, December 13th, 1605-7
Eaton Griffith, V., Oetliker, P. and Oswin, P. (1983) A Time
to Speak, Chest, Heart and Stroke Association, London
Meikle, N., Wechsler, E., Tupper, A., Benenson, M., Butler, J.,
Mulhall, D. and Stern, G. (1979) 'Comparative Trial of
Volunteer and Professional Treatments of Dysphasia after
Stroke', British Medical Journal, July 14th, 87-9

Chapter Nine

A CONTINENCE ADVISORY SERVICE

B. Hamilton

INTRODUCTION

In 1979 a Continence Advisory Service came into being within
South Birmingham Health District. The purpose of this service
is to offer to people living in the community advice on the
promotion of continence or on the management of incontinence,
so that a normal life could be followed.
        To date incontinence is not recognised as a sympton for
which health or social services have to provide statutory help,
whether financial, practical or in the form of aids. Recommendations were made by the DHSS in 1976 advising health authorities to look carefully at the problem of incontinence, and to
ensure that there was further dissemination of information
about this problem, but how this was to be organised was not
defined. The lack of guidelines accounted for variation in the
level of care and help available to incontinent people. In
South Birmingham a working party was set up in 1976 to look at
how best to disseminate information and provide better advice
and care for incontinent persons. The working group identified
a need for one person - a nurse - to act as an advisor on incontinence; and for the improvement and expansion of the
service for the issue of aids to those suffering from incontinence.
        I was appointed as Nursing Sister in charge of the ser-
vice working full time. I was accommodated in the University
Department of Geriatric Medicine with the use of a clinical
room, storage for equipment and paperwork, an examination couch,
and the help of departmental secretarial staff.

SERVICES AVAILABLE TO INCONTINENT PEOPLE IN SOUTH BIRMINGHAM

In 1975, the South Birmingham Department of Community Loans of
Nursing Equipment took over from the local authority an incontinence service catering for 100 persons, who received a laundry
service and disposable products delivered weekly to their
homes. General practitioners, community nurses, health

visitors and social workers could request this service for
their clients. As a result of steadily growing demand, the
service was expanded to provide for 250 persons by 1976 and
for 500 by 1979. At the end of 1979, when the Continence Advisor was in post, there was a waiting list of about 100 persons for this service. No expansion of the service has
occurred since then, despite a further growth in demand, so
that in 1983 there were 500 people receiving supplies and
about 400 people on the waiting list.

The service supplies far more disposable products than it
does bed linen. There are three vans working three days of
the week delivering the aids, and collecting back used laundry
and disposable products that recipients are unable to dispose
of themselves. Fifty per cent of the monies allocated to this
service is spent on administration, storage and deliveries,
and 50 per cent on the aids themselves. When the vans are not
involved on the 'incontinence runs', they are used to deliver
other nursing equipment to patients' homes, such as beds, back
rests and walking frames.

The District Health Authority also provides a loans service for bedpans, urinals and commodes, where it is anticipated that these will be required for not more than three months.
When the aids are required for longer then they are provided
by the Social Services Department of the City of Birmingham.
The latter department is also responsible for alterations that
have to be made in the home, such as fitting a shower or a
downstairs toilet; hand rails to the stairs or toilet frames.

Voluntary organisations help by providing washing machines,
tumble driers and other expensive aids which none of the statutory services normally provide.

The community nursing services provide advice on the
management of incontinence and can order equipment and aids
and provide practical help to those unable to bath themselves
and those requiring enemas and suppositories. The community
nurses are unable to provide a service to those in whom incontinence is the only problem: because of their workload and
possibly because incontinence is not identified as something
nursing staff can do anything about.

Home helps assist incontinent clients by helping with personal washing, fetching aids from chemists and prescriptions
from doctors, and by giving general moral support.

Health visitors and social workers arrange the statutory
services to provide support, day centres for those who require
social contact, community nursing services and home helps for
those who require practical help.

General practitioners can refer incontinent patients to
the appropriate hospital consultant (urologist, gynaecologist,
geriatrician or psychiatrist). The GP can order male urine
collection devices, catheters and drainage bags on FP 10 pre-
scription, and can refer patients to a community nurse for
advice on management, and to order aids from the Nursing

A Continence Advisory Service

Equipment Loans Department.
     Where incontinent persons are on Supplementary Benefit
and incur extra laundering costs in excess of 45p per week, the
DHSS should provide extra funds. An annual special needs
allowance may be claimed to buy the extra clothing and linen
an incontinent person may require, while in exceptional circumstances, soiled mattresses and soft furnishings may be replaced
and a reconditioned washing machine provided. This help is
rarely claimed because people are too embarrassed to tell a
DHSS official about their special need.
     Chemists' shops and mail order firms are further sources
of supply for incontinence aids. The full cost has to be paid
by the patient and no advice is given on which aid is suitable
for which type of incontinence, or on the promotion of continence.

GAPS IN THE SERVICES PROVIDED

The major gaps in the services for the incontinent person in
the community were:

1. Lack of advice to those whose only problem was
    incontinence.
2. The emphasis of the services was on the management of
    incontinence, and very little was being done to pro-
    mote continence, though surgery was available for
    patients with uterine prolapses or enlarged prostate
    glands.
3. Many people who bought their own aids were buying in-
    appropriately and wasting their money.
4. The manufacturers of aids were not receiving the
    information they required to improve their products.
5. Work which was being done by health professionals
    around the district was not disseminated to other
    areas.

DEVELOPMENT OF THE CONTINENCE ADVISORY SERVICE

The main impetus in encouraging health districts to review
their policy on incontinence came from the letter in 1976
drafted by Dame Phyllis Friend, then Chief Nursing Officer at
the DHSS, asking all health districts to look at what services were offered to the incontinent person in the community,
and what steps needed to be taken to improve that service.
     In South Birmingham an application was made to the
District Management Team in 1976 for the appointment of a Nurse
Advisor. A working party was set up to evaluate services within the district. Towards the end of 1978 approval was given
for a two year temporary post to be funded from the West Midlands Regional Health Authority, on condition that monies would
be obtained from a research body to evaluate the role of the

Advisor.

In August 1979 I came into the post, having had six years previous experience in geriatric nursing, as a staff nurse, then ward sister and in-service training officer. I had also previously worked on genito-urinary and gynaecological wards, but had no experience in the community. I had attended a one day seminar on incontinence at the Disabled Living Foundation.

My first two weeks were spent being orientated into the district meeting community nurses, supplies officers, day hospital staff and my new colleagues. The next three months were spent getting to grips with the practicalities of promoting continence, managing incontinence and organising how the service was to be run. It was anticipated that there would be many referrals once the advisor's presence was known, and thus only a few GPs and the community nursing officers were initially informed. I was the third advisor to be appointed in the whole country. I must admit that in 1979 I knew no more about incontinence and its management than the next nurse, and I was a little nervous at the thought of others seeking advice from me. I spent much time searching medical and nursing books and journals in an attempt to improve my knowledge. Unfortunately at that time there were no courses run to help people like myself. Referrals were slow to come in during the first two months because I had no office base, but once I had a telephone number where I could be contacted, I had enough referrals to keep me busy.

The job description I had been given stated that I should provide a service to all incontinent persons within South Birmingham Health District. This was based on the assumption that there were between 500 and 1000 incontinent persons who were already known to the Health and Social Services. However, in 1980 a survey carried out by Thomas et al (1980) showed that there were in the community many people who did not seek help for incontinence, through embarrassment or ignorance that anything could be done. In South Birmingham, which has a population of just over one-quarter of a million, of whom 14 per cent are aged 65 years and over, it is probable that there are 1,500 persons aged 65 years and over and 6,000 persons between 16 and 64 years who suffer from regular urinary and/or faecal incontinence. It therefore became apparent that I was not going to be able to see and help all these people.

THE STARTING OF AN ADVISORY SERVICE

My work comprises: (1) giving advice to incontinent persons and their carers about the promotion of continence and the management of incontinence; (2) working in the Urodynamic Unit, to be described below; and (3) education of health professionals in methods of promoting continence and managing incontinence.

There is no restriction upon who refers an incontinent person to the Advisory Service. Table 9.1 shows the source of referrals to the service over the twelve months to November 1982.

Table 9.1: Source of referral of community patients to Advisory Service, December 1981 to November 1982

Source of referral	Number of Patients	%
General practitioners	74	33
Hospital doctors	47	21
Community nurses/health visitors	25	11
Social workers	13	4
Home helps	20	9
Self	18	8
Other	27	12
Total	224	100

Over 50 per cent of all referrals were from medical sources, 11 per cent from nursing sources and 35 per cent from others.

Table 9.2: Age distribution of referred patients

Age	Number of Patients	%
Under 15 years	18	8
15-29 years	9	4
30-49 years	38	17
50-69 years	62	28
70 and over	97	43
Total	224	100

INITIAL VISIT

The initial visit to see the patient in their own home is usually carried out within six weeks of the referral being made. The time interval between referral and when the patient is first seen does vary, according to my particular workload at

that time, though health professionals who make referrals can
get immediate advice over the telephone at the time of referral. If I anticipate that it may be more than six weeks before a patient can be seen, I advise the referer to contact
their community nurse, who will be able to give initial advice on management of the incontinence, while awaiting my
assessment.

Very active and mentally alert patients may be asked to
visit me rather than receive a home visit. When the patient
is seen for the first time a complete record of urinary and
bowel symptoms is made, together with a full environmental
assessment in relation to **the** person's mobility, dexterity and
mental function. Also noted are the patient's normal daily
activities, attitude towards incontinence and relationships
with other people. A physical examination is made including
abdonimal, rectal and vaginal examination, and a brief neurological examination. Advice is given on fluid and dietary in-
take. The patient is asked to keep a record of when they pass
urine into a toilet or urinal, and when they find themselves
wet. These times are then recorded on the Bladder Record
Chart, which has a separate section for when urine is passed
into the toilet and a section for incontinence. The chart
has seven sections to cover one week and each day is divided
into one-hourly boxes. The patient puts a tick in the appropriate day and hour box when urine is passed either continently
or incontinently (see Appendix A).

The chart gives a far more accurate record than the average person can give in a history, and it is kept for one week
initially to assess the problem. For those people - about 10
per cent - who have involvement with a community nurse, it is
usual for the nurse to be present at this interview and to implement any advice which I give. The next stage is to contact
the GP with the patient's permission, normally by telephone.
I present what I view as the problem and the GP adds any further information which the patient did not furnish. A decision is then made on the patient's management, the options being referral to a hospital consultant, promotion of continence
with toiletting regimens and aids to help toiletting in those
patients with reduced mobility and dexterity; or to the at-
tainment of 'social continence' in those patients where previous attempts at promoting continence have failed. This would
allow the patient to lead as normal a life as possible, with
the use of various collection and absorptive devices.

Patients referred to hospital consultants may be rendered
continent by removal of the prostate gland or by pelvic floor
repair. When a disease process is found, which is not reme-
died by surgery, the patient may be referred back to me with
the aim of promoting social continence. Of 224 patients whom
I assessed in the twelve months to November 1982, 16 were referred to hospital consultants, 141 were selected forthe promotion of continence and in the remaining 67 the aim was for

social continence.

When promotion of continence is aimed for, and the community nurse is not involved, it has proved necessary to undertake between six and twelve visits over a period of up to four months. Apart from implementing a toileting regimen geared to the individual patient, aids may be required to facilitate toileting, or to achieve social continence. Whilst taking part in a toileting regimen, the patient requires a lot of encouragement, particularly on days when things are not going too well, and this is why I make follow-up visits.

Of the 141 patients in whom attempts at promotion of continence were made, 30 per cent became fully continent, 50 per cent found the level of incontinence had reduced, though they were not fully continent and 20 per cent were not helped. When intervention fails or does not reach expectations, then I have further consultation with the GP which may lead to further investigations to confirm the diagnosis.

Where it is felt that continence is not going to be achieved, as in patients living alone, with brain failure and no constant main carer involved on regular daily visits, then social continence is the aim. In this case particularly the community nurses would be involved in an average of three to four follow-up visits to ensure that incontinence aids are issued, that they are suitable for the patient and that they are being managed satisfactorily.

All patients who see me are given my card, so that they can contact me if they have any problems and can also come back once I have discharged them. I am available in my office daily between 9.00 and 10.00 a.m. to receive calls personally.

THE URODYNAMIC UNIT

I am attached to the urodynamic unit as a clinical nurse for two clinics a week, one for urology and one for geriatric medicine, to carry out standard urodynamic tests (e.g. cystometrography urine flow measurements) in selected patients in whom a diagnosis cannot be made on history and physical examination alone, or in whom confirmation of the original diagnosis is required, or where there is doubt as to a diagnosis prior to surgery.

TEACHING

Teaching accounts for about five hours a week. Teaching sessions can be requested by any professional group or organisation involved in helping incontinent people, including student and pupil nurses, qualified nurses, home helps, residential home care staff, student physiotherapists, medical students, GP trainees, social workers and multi-disciplinary groups. Groups of relatives managing incontinence within their own families also request talks. Many health professionals come out with me for a day or half day to see how I work.

My other duties include meeting representatives from companies who sell aids and equipment relating to incontinence, and giving advice on improvement of aids, also producing information for audio-visual aids. Table 9.3 gives a breakdown of how my time was used in the twelve months to November, 1982.

Table 9.3: Continence advice: distribution of work in an average week

	Hours per week	Percentage
Community visits	20	53
Urodynamic clinic	6	16
Administration	5	13
Teaching (formal)	5	13
Other	$1\frac{1}{2}$	5
Total	$37\frac{1}{2}$	100

Attempts were made to hold a nursing clinic in the outpatients department, but this did not work well for three main reasons: (1) ambulances were unreliable in getting patients to the clinic on time, and would often fail to arrive; (2) patients did not always give a true picture of their home circumstances and their way of life, making it necessary for me to do a home visit, which was much more informative; and (3) it was more costly to bring the patient to the clinic than for me to visit the patient's home.

COSTING

The costs of running the Advisory Service in South Birmingham included the following items:

1. Nursing Sister salary.
2. Employer's overheads – National Insurance + superannuation.
3. Travelling costs – average 100 miles a week.
4. Office accommodation – lighting, heating, telephone and stationery.
5. Supply of aids which may not have been incurred otherwise.

EVALUATION

A research nurse was appointed for two years, with funds provided by the British Foundation for Age Research to evaluate the work of the Nurse Advisor. The evaluation comprised an analysis of the work done, based on a diary kept by the Nurse Advisor; and an estimate of its effectiveness.

The activity of the Nurse Advisor in an average week, and the time devoted to her various activities, are summarised in Table 9.4.

Table 9.4:   Activity of Nurse Advisor

Hours devoted to:	home visits	25
	clinic	7.5
	teaching	5
Number of visits per week		33
Miles travelled		112
Time spent per visit (minutes)		45
Of which time with patient		35
	travelling time	10
Travelling distance per visit (miles)		3.7
Number of visits per case treated		5
Cost per visit, including travelling (1981)		£4.13
Approximate average cost per treated patient (including administrative costs)		£25

The effectiveness of the intervention proved difficult to de-termine. The difficulties have been described elsewhere, but since the problem of evaluating new services is very general, the arguments will be repeated here, more briefly (see Badger et al., 1983).

There were two major methodological difficulties: (1) to define, in measurable terms, the objectives of the nurse's in-tervention; (2) to devise a controlled experiment.

Objectives of the Intervention
The original research concept related to the nurse's aim of re-ducing incontinence, and efforts were made to devise methods of measuring whether this had happened. This task is difficult enough in a hospital ward when 24 hour observation can be un-dertaken; but it proved unattainable in the homes of patients. Such terms as 'number of episodes of incontinence','number of times changed' or 'amount of linen used' proved to be either difficult to apply - particularly in inter- rather than intra-patient comparisons - or not directly related to the clinical state. For example, the number of pads used per patient per day measured not, as was hoped, the severity of the inconti-nence, but the availability of supplies and the fastidiousness of helpers. Indeed, in severe instances, the intervention of the nurse led to an increase in the use of pads, and thus bet-ter patient management. It was concluded that the best

measure of effectiveness might be the subjective statements of
patients and helpers about whether benefit had been perceived
in three areas: change in amount of incontinence;   change in
management;   or better benefits from advice given.

Controlled Experiment

Patients and helpers might express appreciation of a visit
whether or not the intervention was effective. A controlled
experiment was therefore undertaken. An 'ideal' research design required the random allocation of referred patients to a
'treatment' or 'no-treatment' group. The recently appointed
Incontinence Nurse Advisor was working very hard to build up
the confidence of general practitioners, community nurses, social workers and, especially patients and their relatives, in
the new service. Thus the idea of introducing a random allocation to determine whether patients, who had put their trust
in the new service, would receive treatment or not, proved
unacceptable. To avoid this difficulty the control group was
drawn from an adjoining health district which had no domiciliary continence advisory service, with the plan that incontinent patients of both groups would be seen by the research
nurse on referral and three months later, when any differences
between the groups in the patients' and relatives' assessment
of benefit could be attributed to the intervention of the
Nurse Advisor.
        Identical criteria for admission to the trial were used,
but subsequent analysis revealed that the 'control' group dif-
fered signficantly from the treatment group in sex and GP
contact in previous month, but were similar in duration and
severity of incontinence.
        That the research was based on unmatched groups did not
frustrate the research intention. The research demonstrated a
significant effect in that one quarter of the control group believed their incontinence had improved in the three month observation period, whereas one half of the 'treatment' group believed they had recovered or improved in the same period. However, the major finding of the study proved to be the feeling
of having been helped, which was expressed by about half the
patients and carers in the 'treatment' group. A few of those
in the control group, who had received no help, expressed
appreciation of the research nurse's visits and said they too
felt they had been helped. The type of comment that was most
frequently encountered in both research groups was: 'It makes
such a difference to talk to someone who really understands'.
Nearly one half of the carers of the 'treatment' group stated
that the advice and equipment which they had received marked-
ly eased the daily problems of managing the patient's incontinence.
        This evidence proved sufficient to convince the Regional
Health Authority of the value of the Service, and, on completion of the research, the decision was made to provide

permanent funding for the post of Continence Advisor.

THE ADVISOR'S OVERVIEW

The research findings were a little disappointing in that a
greater level of patient satisfaction was hoped for. Some reasons may be:

1. The Study was carried out soon after my appointment
   when I did not have enough expertise in solving the
   problems of incontinence.
2. Because I was not a community-trained nurse, there
   was a reluctance amongst some of the nurses to co-
   operate fully with what I was attempting to do.
3. Many of the incontinent patients referred during the
   evaluation period had incontinence of more than one
   year's duration, and they had established coping
   routines which were not easily amenable to change.
4. Patients were referred for the management of incontinence rather than the promotion of continence. This
   may have reflected my original title of 'Specialist
   Nurse Advisor on Incontinence'.

The following changes were made to the Service after September,
1982:

1. My title was changed to Continence Advisor.
2. More time was allocated to formal and informal teaching. Because of the high prevalence of incontinence,
   no one person would be able to help all sufferers, so
   the education of other professionals was essential.
3. The criteria for referrals from health professionals
   were to include evidence that basic investigations,
   assessments and attempts at the promotion of continence or social continence had been undertaken by the
   referring professional.
4. Where referrals were received from non health professions (which is what I feel must continue to take
   place) after the initial assessment has been made, I
   attempt to involve their community nurse to carry
   out follow-ups. To date, no agreement has been
   reached with senior community nurse management that
   community nurses will follow up patients who have
   been referred to the Continence Advisor, but individual nurses may be approached to do so.
5. Where a person is taken on to my caseload for promotion of continence, I always make frequent follow-up
   visits. This has reduced my caseload from 30 to 20
   persons, but has improved the success rate, as only
   one or two pieces of advice are given at each visit.
6. More time is spent on evaluating equipment, so that

recommendations can be made to manufacturers for improvements. This has meant a closer liaison with manufacturers and has improved their understanding of incontinence and of other problems, like reduced mobility and dexterity of some individuals.

FUTURE POLICY

As more people seek help for incontinence now that it is not quite such a taboo subject, and people become aware of better management methods than newspapers on the bed and chair and torn up sheeting placed between the legs, more help will be required.

In my opinion the answer is not to employ a whole team of specialist nurses to deal with this problem, but to select a nurse in each hospital unit and each community area, to undergo a brief training course covering the following topics:

1. Normal micturition.
2. Bladder dysfunction.
3. Nursing assessment.
4. Toiletting regimens
5. Aids to social continence.
6. Faecal incontinence.

At the end of this course the nurse would act as a disseminator of information on incontinence and would have time to make assessments and give advice on the promotion of continence or social continence. If this person was unable to help or if management failed then the patient could be referred to the Continence Advisor. This system would make more nurses responsible for managing the patients in their care and would also act as a filter for patients referred to the Continence Advisor, freeing her to take on a larger caseload or to devote more time to the Urodynamic Clinic. The newly formed English National Board (August 1983) is in the process of approving a two-week course for qualified nurses and I am acting as an advisor to this body.

Moves are afoot to increase the funding for incontinence equipment in the community, and a fresh look is being taken at how these aids are distributed. Maybe more people could collect aids from central points, thus cutting down on delivery costs, or maybe some people would be prepared to buy their aids from an 'incontinence shop' run by the health district. This would benefit manufacturers by obviating the need to deliver small quantities to many places.

An association of Continence Advisors has been formed with a national body which meets for two days a year, and regional groups. The West Midlands regional group has a membership of about 30, with another 15 attending at our ten weekly meetings. Now that there are 18 full time Continence Advisors throughout

the country, it should become easier for new nurses to come
into post. The day will come when all incontinent patients
can get help in the early stages, and the misery that this
complaint causes will be significantly reduced.

POSTSCRIPT

The suggestion made by the Department of Health and Social
Security in 1976, referred to in this article, that a specialist nurse in management of incontinence should be identified
in every health district, although by no means yet fully implemented, is advancing strongly. The specialist nurses in
the UK have banded themselves into an Association in which
they share their experience. The major activities have been
educational in their own health districts and through their
contributions to multi-disciplinary and regional and national
meetings and publications; and the stimulus they have given
to manufacturers in the design and development of new products; and in their group evaluations of the products on the
market. The meetings and publications of the group have attracted international attention, and it seems likely that the
concept of specialisation in the management of the incontinent
patient would spread beyond the United Kingdom. Emphasis is
predominantly on the needs of the elderly (Blannin, 1983);
but attention is also being directed to the needs of other
age groups (Parker, 1983).

NOTE

Thanks are due to Frances Badger for her helpful comments on
an earlier draft of this chapter.

REFERENCES

Badger, F. J., Drummond, M. F. and Isaacs, B. (1983) 'Some
    issues in the clinical, social and economic evaluation
    of new nursing services', Journal of Advanced Nursing,
    8, 481-494
Blannin, J. P. (1983) 'The role of the nurse continence
    adviser', Physiotherapy, 69, 111-2
Parker, G. (1983) 'What makes a good incontinence service?',
    Primary Health Care, September, 11-12
Thomas, T. M., Plymat, K. R., Blannin, J. and Meade, F. W.
    (1980) 'Prevalence of urinary incontinence', British
    Medical Journal, 281, 1243-1245

APPENDIX A: Bladder Record Chart

Week commencing ....   Name ....   Address ....

Enter a tick in appropriate square each time you pass urine normally

Normal

	8am	9am	10am	11am	12 noon	1pm	2pm	3pm	–	–	–	–	–	–	–	–	4am	5am	6am	7am
Mon.																				
Tues.																				
Wed.																				
Thur.																				
Fri.																				
Sat.																				
Sun.																				

Morning   Afternoon   Evening   Night

Enter a tick in appropriate square each time you are wet or damp

Incontinent

	8am	9am	10am	11am	12 noon	1pm	2pm	3pm	–	–	–	–	–	–	–	–	4am	5am	6am	7am
Mon.																				
Tues.																				
Wed.																				
Thur.																				
Fri.																				
Sat.																				
Sun.																				

Special instructions:

Chapter Ten

MAKING A GERIATRIC DEPARTMENT EFFECTIVE

J. F. Harrison

THE INHERITANCE, THE RESPONSIBILITY AND THE AIMS

The British specialty of geriatrics (or 'geriatric medicine')
has ambitious pretensions, customarily expressed as the preventive, social, clinical and remedial aspects of medicine in
old age, and like other medical specialties it emphasises the
importance of research. Yet even in the 1980s, British consultant geriatricians have to contend with the social realities of the National Health Service (NHS) inheritance: nineteenth century workhouses turned into 'chronic sick' wards of
municipal hospitals, turned yet again into NHS geriatric departments. They and their colleagues also have to work alongside all the other hospital specialties which perforce devote large parts of their time and resources to people of retirement age. Associated with this inheritance is the conventional expectation, greater or less according to circumstances,
that when old people become ill and disabled they are eligible
for accommodation away from their own homes and families until
they die, however long the duration and wherever the accommodation may be.
      Until fairly recently the usual geriatric approach has
been to concentrate on improving accommodation by reducing bed
numbers and by upgrading, rebuilding and/or resiting wards as
appropriate; to place emphasis on 'assessment', rehabilitation and day hospitals, and to exclude from long stay at least
those people whose disabilities are relatively mild. Such
programmes however tend to exclude all but a few emergency admissions. The department usually has a waiting list, so that
when old people are referred to hospital because of medical
crises they are most likely to be dealt with by other specialties which then perceive the geriatric service simply as a
long-term refuge of last resort. The department's experiences
are different from those of mainstream medical thinking, and
mutual misunderstandings persist. Relatively low staffing levels and large numbers of untrained staff are all it can
achieve; recently-qualified doctors, nurses and therapists

are reluctant to enter the specialty, and indeed junior medical posts may be found unsuitable for training. Worst of all, the word 'geriatric' becomes indelibly associated with hopeless decrepitude.

In the mid-1970s however there was an upsurge of public and political interest in 'the problem of the elderly', arising directly from the arithmetic of demography: there would either have to be a massive increase in hospital or other residential accommodation or current practices would have to change. Results included a big increase in local authority (LA) domiciliary services, compulsory inclusion of geriatrics in State Registered Nurse training, a new interest in the specialty by the Royal Colleges of Physicians and General Practitioners, establishment of chairs of geriatric medicine in many medical schools, and greater interests too from the now-growing number of British medical graduates. Nevertheless, even in 1975 the local (Birmingham) prestige of geriatrics in medical circles was not high, and many of us believed that the new Chair of Geriatric Medicine at Birmingham University would not by itself put the situation right. The academic department had a massive educational task to face, but unless the operating policies of the NHS department with which it was to be linked were also seen to be enlightened, criticism of the specialty would not abate.

If the ensuing account seems to concentrate on issues of policy and management almost to the exclusion of standards of patient care, it should be realised that the latter were not in question. There was certainly no reason to criticise the NHS department's existing medical competence nor its concern for patients as people needing help. There were however grounds for believing that whatever improvements in service to individuals might be desirable, and might in fact be made, would depend on the implementation of a new strategy for the department as a whole. There was also no question of empire-building: a considerable empire had been inherited and the problem was how to run it.

Without doubt the NHS consultants had a key role, not in formal management but in determining (consciously or not) the department's operating policies; they had and still have the principal responsibility for deciding who is admitted to or discharged from the hospital wards in which they work, though their decisions do not go unchallenged and they are not necessarily personally involved in every case. They were and are intensely conscious of conflicting pressures for admission and often against discharge, from NHS hospital medical and surgical colleagues, from patients' relatives and other supporters, from community social and nursing services and family doctors, from local authority and independent residential homes and sheltered housing, from NHS psychiatric services, and relatively rarely from patients themselves. Conversely they are aware that the staff of their own department

are also justifiably concerned about the nature and quantity
of their own work load.

In resolving these conflicts the consultants have to understand and evaluate each set of interests and each opinion,
relying on the mutual confidence of all the parties concerned
(which may take time and effort to build up) but even more on
expert understanding of their patients' illnesses, disabilities, degrees of real dependency, and prognoses. Given the
assumption that institutional residential care (IRC) may be on
offer somewhere, whether in hospital or a so-called residential
home, in ordinary clinical practice it is perpetually evident
that demand for this commodity is far greater than could be delivered by beds available in the geriatric department alone
(currently in Birmingham nine per 1000 population over the age
of 65 (1). If the department is to fulfil any role other than
that of last-resort refuge and is to give any kind of prompt
service, selection for the 'privilege' of IRC has to be conscious, rigorous, and if necessary, innovatory.

Within this framework of thinking, with the arrival in
South Birmingham of a new team of consultant geriatricians in
1975-78 a number of objectives were set, all of them on the
assumption that there would be little or no increase in money
resources. The South Birmingham department was however already
reasonably well endowed. It had a nearly-defined catchment
area, and besides the number of beds indicated above it had
quite generous day-hospital provision, although only 23 per
cent of the beds and 28 per cent of the day places were on a
district general hospital (DGH) site. The establishment of
junior doctors, remedial therapists and social workers was
mostly adequate and there were several general practitioner
(GP) assistants, although none of the junior medical posts was
approved for professional training. The practice of domiciliary visiting by consultants was well established. The annual
patient throughput per bed was, however, only a little over
two, and very few wards had any designated special function.
There was (and remains) no specialised psychiatric service for
old people and a report in 1974 had criticised the department
for accepting too great a share of responsibility for ambulant
patients with mental infirmity.

Although the 1975-78 objectives were not consciously enu-
merated at the time, they may be listed as follows:

1. To abolish the waiting list and to give priority at
   all times to dealing promptly with requests for help.
2. To adjust the work load so as to attract competent,
   well-motivated clinical staff throughout the department.
3. To establish friendly, mutually satisfactory working
   relationships with all other agencies and services
   which are involved with the same people and problems.
4. To diffuse responsibility and experience as evenly as

possible throughout the four units and 19 wards of
the department, so as to create widespread understanding of problems and priorities and to distribute
the task of decision making.

5.   To ensure that every patient has a clearly defined
programme of objectives which will be followed
through to its conclusion.

6.   While making every effort to reduce the commitment
to IRC, to participate as far as possible in all fea-
sible alternative systems of support and care, especially programmes of planned short stay (PSS).

Before a description of some of the methods adopted to achieve
these objectives, some further comment on relevant local factors is needed. The catchment area is now precisely defined
(about 36 square miles) and entirely urban; about 40 per cent
of the housing stock is municipally owned, and housing standards are generally at least adequate. The area comprises
the whole of one (South Birmingham) and most of another
(Central Birmingham) NHS district, from 1st April 1974 to
1st April 1982 under Birmingham Area Health Authority but since
then under two separate district health authorities. Social
services and housing are managed by a single local authority;
NHS ambulance transport is provided by the regional health
authority. Three DGHs principally serve the area; in the
South District one DGH deals with most of the hospital referrals and has rather a small department of medicine, but in the
Central District the two DGHs undertake city-wide and regional
responsibilities, sharing a much larger department of medicine.
There is no medical rehabilitation specialty. A 16-bed NHS
unit for younger disabled people, served by one of the geriatricians, accepts referrals from further afield than the geriatric catchment area alone.

A conspicuous feature of the department is the deliberate
provision of 60 per cent of its beds in buildings erected between 1964 and 1972, replacing old workhouse accommodation but
all on peripheral sites - that is, in wholly geriatric hospitals which are however within the catchment area and are well
provided with routine laboratory, radiology, remedial-therapy
and social work services. Three full time consultant geriatricians were at first responsible for more than 450 beds, although one ward was subsequently allocated to the new Professor
of geriatric medicine; three physicians with part time responsibilities to geriatrics had the care of three more wards
(about 90 beds), one of which passed to the professorial unit
after a couple of years.

IMPLEMENTING CHANGES

The six objectives set out above were, with the exception of
the PSS programme which was begun two years later, all pursued

together from mid-1975; they were implemented by a number of devices and procedures, many of which served several objectives simultaneously. An important preliminary was to discover what could be learnt about existing practice and in particular to recognise that the largest unit (lately a chest hospital and containing nearly half the beds) was scarcely developed along geriatric lines at all, conventional or unconventional. Reorganisation would clearly involve the co-operation of senior managers: one of the consultants was elected 'chairman of division' by his medical colleagues, and he convened a somewhat inappropriately-named 'management team' of non-medical colleagues (in administration, nursing, physiotherapy, occupational therapy and social work). The responsibilities possessed by these six people were very different and were not even coterminous, but they had in common the important fact of involvement in the department's operating policies. It was essential that major policy changes were discussed by a group of this kind.

Another top level initiative was the so-called health care planning team for the elderly. Set up in an advisory capacity under provisions made by the 1974 NHS reorganisation, it was a multi-disciplinary group chaired, as it happened, in successive years by two of the senior geriatricians. It became a committee in which priorities for the tiny sums allocated for budget expansion were settled, but much more significantly it was a forum in which all the issues of shared responsibility between the services (geriatrics,psychiatry, other hospital specialties, community nursing, general practice, social services, the voluntary sector) were thoroughly and informatively debated. In particular, the team issued carefully-considered recommendations about services for those mentally infirm old people whose physical health is too good to justify involvement by the geriatric department. At the time of writing (1983) some of these recommendations have been implemented although much remains to be done. Since the 1982 NHS reorganisation the work of the team has been continued in two separate planning groups, one for each district.

To return to the six objectives: one task was quite easily accomplished. Domiciliary consultations had previously been carried out at any time up to two weeks after being requested by GPs, and were commonly regarded as pre-requisites for the admission of all patients not previously known to the department. The new team resolved to carry out as many visits as possible within 48 hours of receiving each request, and they also decided to ask their junior medical colleagues to help if the load at any particular time became too great. Although unorthodox this was quite logical: junior hospital doctors have always had to take decision making responsibilities, and in any case many if not most of those likely to work in the department would be planning to enter general practice. They were urged to discuss their visits with their consultants afterwards so

that any important action was jointly decided. The consultants
also made known that any bona fide emergency admission was welcome if a GP considered it necessary and if a bed was available
– which at first was all too infrequent. It was essentially a
matter of mutual trust, but it was also based on reality: if
the geriatric department refused an essential admission the
patient would simply turn up in another hospital department,
and if there were subsequent difficulties with discharge the
geriatric service would have to be involved in any case. But
it is common experience that most illnesses causing emergency
admission are resolved quite quickly, and indeed it is incon-
sistent to urge the importance of prevention if prompt response to a crisis is not considered important.

The next step was to get rid of the waiting list, which
could obviously be done either by speeding up the rate of discharge so that patients might be more readily admitted, or by
reducing the number of promises to admit. The second procedure could be applied much more quickly and was put into
effect at once. Admission requests from the community were
refused if there was no serious physical illness, and undertaking admission with no view to discharge was a practice
which virtually ceased. People who had learnt to expect a
different response were naturally distressed and at times there
were angry confrontations; the client group most affected was
that of the ambulant mentally infirm for whom the local psychiatric and social services had been making inadequate provision. Thus calculated political pressure was exerted on
those services within the framework of recognised national
guidelines. Admission requests were further limited by precisely defining the catchment area with the mutual agreement
of colleagues in neighbouring geriatric services, and by making plain that admission 'as a favour' would not be considered.

Requests for transfer from hospital wards were treated
differently. On the assumption that most referrals were for
removal purposes and not for a professional opinion, it was
calculated that a firm promise to transfer at a particular
time would avoid much time-wasting 'consultation' and invi-
dious, arbitrary decision making. There is abundant evidence
that most old people, if they are to be discharged from hospital at all, return home within three months, and there is an
appreciable mortality within the first few weeks of admission.
It was explained to the hospital physicians that there was no
hope of transfers to the geriatric department simply and immediately on demand; that a good geriatric service depended on
attracting good staff, which depended on the work they would
be asked to do; and that there would be a much more equitable
balance if a few people were to remain in general wards so that
vacant beds in the geriatric department should be available
for geriatric emergencies which the general wards would otherwise be expected to admit. On the other hand it was appreciated that vague promises about transfer simply put planning

blight on patients' management, so a firm undertaking was made that eligible patients would not be accepted for transfer in less than two months from admission but would with near certainty be moved in three months. A more generous policy was extended to the much smaller number of potential referrals from surgical wards, and prompt transfer (a practice already locally established) was advocated for patients recovering from trauma, especially fractures of the femoral neck. Patients recently treated in the geriatric department would always be taken back promptly.

Moreover, although referrals from hospital and community could still be made to a particular consultant, colleagues were encouraged to refer each new case simply to the department which would then sort out (on the basis of a regular rota) which consultant would accept it. A direct result of all the procedures described so far was the weekly admission case conference which has now been a regular fixture in the department for more than seven years. At each conference all hospital transfers and all problematic non-urgent community referrals are discussed round a table by all the department's doctors together, with secretarial support. If an admission request is refused, alternative courses of action are usually suggested. Decision making is greatly assisted by the full participation of specialist geriatric health visitors who frequently contribute both valuable information and practical help, and by other groups including nurses and remedial therapists. The conferences have been more effective than almost any other procedure in keeping the waiting list at zero and in generating a consistent, well-informed operational policy throughout the department.

Once the pressure of the waiting list had been removed, renewed efforts could be made towards the emergency admissions which the department had previously been unable or unwilling to take. The aim was not to take every patient over a certain age, but for the geriatric service to pull its weight and acquire sufficient clinical interest to encourage people to work in it. Within the South District DGH, where 23 per cent of the geriatric beds were, arrangements were fairly easy: empty beds in the geriatric wards were simply added to the pool of available medical beds on any given day, with the following instructions:

1. non-surgical patients aged 75 and over should be offered first to the geriatric department and only admitted to general wards if no geriatric bed was available.
2. patients aged 65-74 would be accepted if a geriatric bed but no medical bed was available.
3. patients aged less than 65 were not acceptable as emergencies.

There were inevitable problems with mentally infirm old people who were otherwise well, and a prevalent practice of referring so-called 'social problems' among younger people had to be stopped. Once it was understood, however (and this took a little time) the procedure worked well. Since there were no geriatric beds in the two Central District DGHs, similar arrangements could not be made there.

At this stage the attraction of good junior medical and remedial therapy staff became crucial. They would only be interested if there was adequate clinical experience, but there could be no justification for the admission of emergencies unless patients were dealt with at least as well as on the medical wards. The two developments had to go hand in hand. Together with assurances of clinical interest on the wards and in day hospital and out-patient clinics, the promise was made that the two existing senior house officers (SHOs: one to three years post-qualification) at the DGH would be asked to be involved in domiciliary assessment and follow-up. The arrangements were enough to secure approval for general professional training, and only after that could it be agreed that one of the posts would be included in a vocational training scheme. The remedial therapy and social work input followed along similar lines: the posts became popular once it was realised that there were problems to be solved which were capable of solution.

It soon became apparent that the direct admission policy had real advantages for the patients concerned, notably the mutual confidence which developed when transfer from an 'acute' ward was avoided, and almost certainly the greater sympathy and more appropriate expertise of staff whose responsibilities were entirely devoted to old people. Anxieties sometimes expressed about admission to a ward labelled as geriatric soon subsided when the quality of treatment and care was appreciated.

It was now time to turn attention to the peripheral units which accommodated 77 per cent of the beds. Just as the DGH geriatric wards preferred not to be decanting units from the department of medicine, so also the nursing and remedial therapy staff in the periphery made it quite plain that they felt the same about their relationship to the geriatric unit at the DGH. It was therefore agreed in principle that all four units would be treated the same, none of them being designated purely for rehabilitation or continuing care. This had two obvious advantages: inter-hospital transfers would be minimised and vacant beds could be put into use much sooner. It also seemed that by giving every unit the experience of acute illness in previously healthy old people, of pressures for admission and of procedures for discharge back home, patients would be far less likely to remain in hospital because of failure to grasp the real priorities or simply because of sheer inertia. Within the large unreformed unit this was a particular challenge, especially since the remedial therapists declared that they could not work on every ward (of which there were nine). Emergency admissions to this unit were therefore concentrated at first in three wards (in the oldest buildings) but were not altogether excluded from the others, and the ultimate objective was the all-purpose use of the whole hospital.

The three full-time NHS consultants also had to decide how to deploy themselves. It would have been easy to divide the department into blocks of four or five wards per consultant, but there was felt to be a real danger of separate empires with ultimately incompatible policies. Instead the traditional DGH model of medical firms and shared wards was followed, but on a large scale and implemented in several stages. Among their fifteen wards the three consultants work together in five and two of them work together in seven, the other three wards having one consultant each. Each consultant's firm consists of a junior doctor or GP assistant, physiotherapist, occupational therapist and social worker, and each of these may or may not be shared with other firms. The network of arrangements has the double effect of spreading expertise throughout the department and of allowing staff to compare each other's methods, while providing clear clinical accountability within each firm. It is a time-honoured system in prestigious hospitals so its effectiveness in a geriatric department is scarcely surprising. The price paid by the consultants, of having to visit ten or eleven wards in four units, is generally agreed to be justified by the flexibility and responsiveness which the system generates.

Establishing the firms meant that programmes of initial management, further assessment, rehabilitation and further support as appropriate, could be devised for all the patients as soon as they were admitted. Members of each firm learned to work together as a matter of routine, and every week on every ward each firm was able to hold its own ward round and/or case conference. The regular meeting between key members of the team was and remains crucially important: each firm has developed its own style of conducting business, but the central objective of communicating with one another and never losing sight of any patient's agreed goal is the key to the first component of keeping the waiting list at zero: ensuring prompt discharge whenever it becomes possible. Moreover, continuity of care was also established as a principle; it was agreed that re-referrals and re-admissions should whenever possible go back to the firm that previously looked after them, and that any patient seen by a member of the firm at home or in a clinic should be admitted to one of his or her firm's beds. The shared-ward concept greatly helped this principle to operate.

The new firms also meant that the junior medical posts in the periphery could be made suitable for general professional training like those at the DGH. There were however particular difficulties in each unit. In one of them the problem was solved by bringing its SHO into the DGH team and then asking all three SHOs to cover the peripheral unit, which was three miles away, as part of their duties. In another unit the development of training posts was considered impracticable, so the existing registrar post (usually three to five years post-qualification) was converted to the non-training grade of medical assistant (2) to allow the occupant to remain working alongside his GP assistant colleagues. The 'undeveloped' unit again presented the greatest challenge: it had been accustomed to resident medical cover from two registrars and an SHO, helped by three GP assistants. Stage by stage the GP assistants were increased to five, the registrars were withdrawn, and another SHO was added. The two SHOs were expected to be at the DGH once every five days to help in emergency cover there, to attend training courses as appropriate, and to be involved in domiciliary work as well: the unit therefore, like the others, had to learn to accept non-resident cover for much of the time.

This particular issue generated many anxieties which had patiently to be allayed. Nurses had to be reminded that even when emergency cases are being regularly admitted, emergencies in a geriatric department are scarcely ever as urgent as those which are common in the general wards of a DGH; that real emergencies always would be attended to by someone who was accessible even if he or she was not in the hospital at every moment; that many emergency calls the nurses had become used to making were not justified at all; that most patients, no matter how ill they might be, were admitted primarily because of social pressures without which they would have been in their own homes with GP cover in the usual way; and that to have a good non-resident doctor was far better than a doctor who was always around but frustrated because of the restrictions on his or her movement and the unsuitability of the post for professional training. Assurances were given that certain kinds of medical emergency (notably profuse gastro-intestinal bleeding) would not be admitted, and eventually the truth of all these propositions became appreciated. The two peripheral SHO posts are now included in a vocational training programme for general practice, leaving two of the three DGH-based SHO posts to be included in training programmes for hospital medicine. The other DGH post was deliberately left out of any such scheme and has consistently attracted good candidates.

The NHS firms have also had the services of a senior registrar (SR : training grade for consultant level) who has usually been attached to one or two firms at a time. The department believes that training for geriatrics is best carried out at SHO and SR grade in the specialty but at registrar grade in general medicine. It has therefore dispensed with its registrar posts and has been allowed to create a sixth SHO post, which has been attached to the professorial firm.

Another initiative was the establishment of fortnightly

meetings with representatives of the social services department to discuss referrals to and from that department's residential homes. Previously a highly inflexible system had operated: patients could only be transferred from hospital to a home if someone else, considered by the home to have become too dependent to be managed there, was accepted in exchange. More urgent referrals from the home for medical reasons were often not taken back if their hospital stay lasted more than three weeks. Visits by hospital staff to the residential homes were very infrequent. Both sides wanted reform, and it was mutually agreed that residents in the local authority homes should be treated by the geriatric department exactly like people in their own homes, with prior 'domiciliary' assessment if necessary and much greater discretion about the length of hospital stay. The fortnightly meetings allowed a valuable exchange of ideas, priorities and problems; the visits to residential homes coupled with a prompt response whenever the geriatric service was really needed did much to establish personal contacts and mutual understanding. Within this framework the principle of exchange still operates, but the department is also offered 35-40 residential places annually without insistence on exchange.

Meanwhile, another development took place which had not been anticipated: pressure from nursing managers and unions and failure of recruitment in one unit led successively to a 9 per cent reduction in available beds. There was however no identifiable lasting effect on the rate of admissions.

After about two years of the new regime and with a third replacement consultant in post, attention was directed to developing programmes of planned short stay (PSS). 'Holiday' admissions had been a feature of the department for some years: every year a family could ask for a relative to be accommodated while they took their summer holiday, and beds were reserved for the purpose between May and September. Often however these admissions became the occasion for the family to insist on long-term hospital care. It seemed obvious that for any severe degree of dependency the hospital service should be planning for more than just an annual admission, even though day hospital attendances might also be available to give relief. Moreover the social services department was developing its own holiday relief scheme, for which the less dependent people were far more appropriate.

The first step was to make the booked fortnights available throughout the year. Spare clerical time was available at a peripheral unit to arrange the bookings. Admissions could be at any interval from every twelve weeks to alternate fortnights, and occasionally periods of more or less than two weeks could be booked. It was soon evident that if the scheme was to work well the full involvement of the relevant consultant and his firm would be needed, to lose no opportunity for assessment, treatment or rehabilitation and to ensure that mutual confidence between the hospital team and supporters at home was established and maintained. It became a part of the service in which continuity of clinical responsibility was of the utmost importance. Beds were progressively made available, distributed among the wards of the peripheral units and reserved exclusively for PSS, up to the current number of about 7 per cent of the department's total.

An alternative programme of PSS was also developed, based on the fortnightly admission of two or three nights which has operated for many years in Oxford. For some reason this proved less popular than the one which was based on longer admissions, although a few patients made use of it. Recently however it has been modified to help in the support of very seriously physically disabled people, simply by offering two or three nights every week. The appreciation shown by patients and their supporters has been most encouraging, and a further 2 per cent of the department's beds are currently reserved for the purpose.

Besides the necessary involvement of the clinical firm, the office support for the PSS programmes has to be well-informed, sympathetic and responsive; time has to be allowed for negotiations of all kinds and for giving advice when it is sought. PSS is also valuable for the traditional geriatric task of assessment: indeed, many patients do not return to hospital after their initial fortnight's stay. The department does not believe it has yet explored the full potential of the various schemes, and this aspect of its service continues to grow. Making beds available is hardly a problem; the resources of the ambulance service and office time have in practice been greater restraints.

The net result of all the developments described so far has been to raise the threshold of disability and social isolation previously considered necessary to justify long-term residence in hospital. The share-out of emergency admissions between the department and the DGH medical wards (two to one over the age of 75) has reached equilibrium, although inequality between the two health districts persists. The department's ability to respond promptly when asked to do so has hardly ever been jeopardised; therefore, as by English standards it is fairly well provided with beds, it has been able to accept that some 45 per cent of its in-patients have been in hospital for six months or more. It follows that an appreciable further proportion, though not having yet stayed for six months, will ultimately do so. This residual component of IRC is therefore large and, since the attentions of the clinical firms are fully taken up with the 'turnover' aspect of the department's work, the long-term residents might be seen to suffer in consequence. In fact they are very largely dependent on the enthusiasm, sympathy and expertise of the nursing staff (which includes a large proportion of untrained auxiliaries) and the role of medicine in this task has never been satisfactorily defined.

Aware however that deliberately mixing IRC with the other components of geriatrics may not be the best option, the department has from time to time considered creating wards with special expertise in IRC. The advantages have so far however seemed elusive. Among the long-term residents there are two main groups: those with severe disorders of the nervous system and those with multiple sources of disability. In both groups two disorders of the brain dominate to the extent that one or other (or both) is present in nearly three-quarters of the residents: they are cerebrovascular disease and senile dementia of the Alzheimer type. A relatively tiny group is severely physically handicapped (for example by orthopaedic failures, rheumatoid arthritis or spinal cord lesions) but mentally normal. One ward has been set aside to provide a more acceptable environment for people of this kind. Our belief however is that to concentrate severely disabled old people together, just because they have no prospect of discharge, is likely to produce more unhappiness than our current policy of desegregation, at any rate within the framework of the medical model.

Finally, little change has been made in the already-existing day hospital service. It provides short-term and long-term support in about equal proportions and has certainly been a most valuable adjunct to the other activities.

AN OUTLINE OF THE RESULTS AND THE FUTURE

Systematic evaluation of the effects of all the initiatives described would be a difficult task which, for reasons of time and availability of personnel, has not been done. Some basic arithmetic concerning work-load is known: an annual admission rate of 1200 in 1975 has been converted to 3600 in 1982. Otherwise it is only possible to set down a few of the reactions of which the department is aware. A consultant's view of these is however necessarily biased, not least because of his own responsibility for many of the policies.

Support from professional colleagues has on the whole been enthusiastic. GPs have appreciated the prompt service; hospital physicians have accepted their part of the deal knowing that it has been made in good faith. Junior doctors have appreciated the experience offered them and the Royal Colleges have been complimentary about it. Remedial therapists and social workers have enjoyed their active role; the ward nursing staff have all liked the greater turnover and the acceptance of patients direct from their homes. Health visitors and community nurses at least know they can work with us and, however firm we may have to be on occasions, they know we will not let them down in a crisis. Relationships with the social services department, despite a few disagreements, have been friendly and constructive. One or two politicians with firm ideas about IRC have objected to our policy about reducing our share of it. Response from the people that matter, patients and their families and friends, is much harder to assess on any but an individual basis. One can only make a personal statement that the overwhelming majority seem greatly appreciative and that it has been a pleasure to work with almost all of them.

The most important potential source of disagreement has been when people have been asked to accept a role change. Initial quarrels have in most instances given way to rueful consideration and then perhaps some hard bargaining, with a final acceptance of a new position on both sides. The local authority residential homes were very reluctant to accept residents with dementia or even the slightest incontinence, and they imagined that they could always send their most dependent residents to the geriatric department for continuing care. They have changed their outlook, but we in turn had to learn the reasonable limits within which they can be expected to do their work. Similarly the community nurses and home helps have had to accept that we will send quite severely disabled people home, but they know this is to make way for others who urgently need our help. Our own nurses and nursing auxiliaries noticed an increasing work load: hence the pressures to reduce beds, which the consultants had to acknowledge. Relationships with the psychiatric service have been difficult because of local medical politics, but at least a modus vivendi has been hammered out which does not depend on the geriatric department doing psychiatric work because, as the GP would tell us, 'We can never get anything out of them'.

In future there will no doubt be continuing change. There are moves to identify a separate service for the Central District which will involve splitting the department, but it will at least provide geriatric beds in the two DGHs there and another consultant post, with a welcome reduction in the present consultants' bed holding. If the large, over-centralised social services department could also localise its services within the city's five health districts, effective partnership would almost certainly be easier to implement. The potential of community support for severely disabled old people has almost certainly not been fully explored locally, and senile dementia presents the most pressing challenge. Individual patients' needs usually change as senile dementia advances, and if only for this reason they present themselves to different services (social, psychiatric, geriatric) at different phases of their illness. None of the services therefore has a clear picture of the magnitude or full nature of dependency due to dementia, and all could improve the responsiveness of what they have to offer if they had better information. Epidemiological investigation of other disabling diseases too, notably strokes, would almost certainly indicate more clearly what should be done to help. Then there is the challenge of IRC:

greater understanding is needed of its objective, limitations and potential. Could not IRC be taken however, by national legislation, out of the NHS altogether? The medical model and the hospital ward concept are both inappropriate to what should be in essence the provision of a domestic environment. It would be far better that local authorities should assume administrative responsibility and contract with local geriatric departments for the expert services they need.

SUMMARY

If the initiatives described in this chapter had depended on waiting for new money, nothing would have happened. Few of them have been innovatory in any other than the local sense, and are better described as management changes incorporating ideas already implemented elsewhere. Just possibly four items come close to being real innovations: the weekly admission case conference, employing junior doctors for domiciliary assessment, admitting emergencies to mixed function wards in peripheral hospitals, and planned short stay of two or three nights each week. These four however are only part of what is intended to be a coherent whole, providing a framework within which the time and skills of the doctors, nurses and therapists can be employed to the best possible advantage of the ill and disabled old people in the catchment area they serve. To have worked within this framework has been arduous but most satisfying: clinicians who enjoy their work are likely to do it well and in so doing to have satisfied patients, not to mention colleagues who appreciate their contribution. In our department we have been conscious of giving satisfaction: possibly there is no better way of judging whether our service has been effective.

POSTSCRIPT: THE WIDER CONTEXT

It is probably not too much to claim that the implementation of policy and practice described in this chapter exemplifies the predicament of British geriatric medicine as a whole, needing as it does to identify itself as a valid and satisfying medical specialty while using its inherited state-financed resources to the best possible advantage of the society it serves. Where there is no geriatric medical specialty different procedures are likely to emerge. Pressures for IRC also vary with differences of religion, culture, wealth, social structure, expectations and prevalence of disability in different communities. A large private sector is also a crucial factor in many parts of the world. Recent British legislation has encouraged the growth of private nursing homes and rest homes financed by the social security benefits of their potential residents. This is already adding an important third component to the local range of services provided by the local authorities, the voluntary services and the NHS, and also the ultimate effect on the distribution of responsibilities as yet can only be conjectured.

Within the United Kingdom the objectives and practices of individual NHS geriatric departments vary greatly from one to another (Silver, 1978; Evans, 1981; Pathy, 1982). In South Birmingham some of these have been consciously based on the strictly age-related, high turnover services developed in Hull (Bagnall et al, 1977; Horrocks, 1983). The reports from Hull are however guarded about the extent to which high turnover benefits people with irremediable dependency, not to mention the extent to which responsibility for IRC is being passed to other agencies and on what terms. Other geriatricians have called for renewed emphasis on the issues of disability and dependency (Millard, 1983) and indeed British geriatrics has yet to decide how far it is the general medicine of old age on the one hand and the specialist medicine of disabling disease on the other (Harrison, 1981). 'Respite care', 'shared care', or PSS as it is referred to in this chapter, is now frequent in many homes and hospitals which cater for people with physical and mental disabilities. The weekly admission scheme described here was developed locally but (as already noted) was based on a report from Oxford (Griffiths and Cosin, 1976). The practical aspects of reorganising old geriatric services and setting up new ones have been set out in other accounts (Jolley et al 1982; Leeming, 1982). To date however South Birmingham has lagged behind the best possible practices of collaboration between geriatrics and psychiatry (Godber, 1978) and there has been no local, coherent community-based policy for the management of dementia, to which attention has repeatedly been drawn as the dominant, most challenging disability in an ageing population (Jolley and Arie, 1980). South Birmingham geriatrics in general seems to be somewhat between the 'custodial' and 'high turnover' ends of the policy continuum, with at least some bias towards higher turnover, and its current practices represent its own compromise with its own local circumstances and conflicting expectations.

NOTES

1. 1981 census figures.
2. Now redesignated 'associate specialist'.

REFERENCES

Bagnall, W. E., Datta, S. R., Knox, J. and Horrocks, P. (1977) 'Geriatric Medicine in Hull: A comprehensive service', British Medical Journal, 1, 102-4

Evans, J. G. (1981) 'Institutional Care', in T. Arie (ed.) Health Care of the Elderly, Croom Helm, London, pp.176-93

Godber, C. (1978) 'Conflict and Collaboration Between Geriatric Medicine and Psychiatry', in B. Isaacs (ed.),Recent Advances in Geriatric Medicine, Churchill Livingstone, Edinburgh, Vol. I, pp. 131-42

Griffiths, R. A. and Cosin, L. Z. (1976) 'The Floating-Bed', Lancet, I, 684-5

Harrison, J. F. (1982) 'Geriatric Medicine and Disabled Living', British Medical Journal, 283, 1096-8

Horrocks, P. (1982) 'The Case for Geriatric Medicine as an Age-Related Specialty', in B. Isaacs (ed.), Recent Advances in Geriatric Medicine, Churchill Livingstone, Edinburgh, Vol. 2, pp. 259-77

Jolley, D. and Arie, T. (1980) 'Dementia in Old Age: An outline of current issues', Health Trends, 12, 1-4

Jolley, D., Smith, P., Billington, L., Ainsworth, D. and Ring, L. (1982) 'Developing a Psychogeriatric Service', in D. Coakley (ed.), Establishing a Geriatric Service, Croom Helm, London, pp. 149-65

Leeming, J. T. (1982) 'Attitudes, Teamwork, Co-ordination and Communication', in D. Coakley (ed.), Establishing a Geriatric Service,Croom Helm, London, pp. 113-31

Millard, P. (1983) 'Should Geriatric Medicine Exist as a Specialty?' Margory Warren Memorial Lecture, delivered to British Geriatric Society on 17th November

Silver, C. P. (1978) 'Patterns of Delivery in Care by Departments of Geriatric Medicine', in. B. Isaacs (ed.), Recent Advances in Geriatric Medicine, Churchill Livingstone, Edinburgh, Vol. I, pp. 121-30

Chapter Eleven

HOLLYMOOR PSYCHOGERIATRIC SERVICE

D. Gaspar

BACKGROUND - MENTAL ILLNESS IN OLD AGE

There is a high prevalence of mental illness in old age, both
of organic mental illness, also known as brain failure, dementia and organic psycho-syndrome, and of functional mental illness; depression, paraphrenia, mania, personality conflict
leading to anxiety, hysteria and prolonged bereavement reaction (Kay, Beamish and Roth, 1964; Bergmann, 1979; Office of
Health Economics, 1979). There are in addition schizophrenics
whose illness started in adulthood and who enter old age with
the disease still active or inactive, but with the personality
much damaged.
    Dementia poses the biggest problem to the Health and
Social Services since 10 per cent of all old people suffer from
dementia (Office of Health Economics, 1979) and since one-
seventh of the population are elderly, a general practitioner
with an average practice may have as many as 25 demented patients known to him (Fuller, Ward, Evans, Massam and Gardner,
1979). Some of these have severe physical illnesses. In
others there are no physical limitations, but behaviour problems loom large. Caring for demented patients forms the core
function of a psychogeriatric service.

POLICY RECOMMENDATIONS

In 1971 the Department of Health and Social Security issued
guidelines relating to psychogeriatric services (DHSS, 1971).
In the following year a more elaborate memorandum was issued
(DHSS, 1972). Besides giving norms in relation to the number
of beds and day places for different categories of mental illness, this document provided the stimulus for psychiatric
hospitals to organise specialist services for mental illness
in old age. Such a service was established at Hollymoor
Hospital, Birmingham. In this chapter the origin and development of that service will be described.

HOLLYMOOR - THE LOCAL SCENE

Hollymoor Hospital is situated in the south-western corner of
the city of Birmingham. It serves a catchment area of 270,000
population in the eastern part of Birmingham and the adjoining
Borough of Solihull. The distance from the hospital to the
catchment area is between eleven and 18 miles. This is not the
ideal setting of a hospital for the practice of assessing patients at home, or for running to see a family at moments of
crisis. Recently the geographical difficulties of the hospital have been slightly eased by the establishment of outpatient
and day patient facilities at East Birmingham Hospital , which
lies on the edge of the catchment area.
    Until 1976 psychiatric services at the hospital were
supplied by five consultant psychiatrists, of whom I was one.
We provided a service for patients of all ages in a geographi-
cally defined sector. When a patient with dementia was referred, the appropriate sector consultant sought a bed in one
of the 'psychogeriatric' wards, which were used as long-stay
units only. This purely custodial system was unsatisfactory.
The retirement in 1976 of a physician in geriatric medicine
who had part-time responsibilities and two wards at Hollymoor
Hospital, provided me with the opportunity of changing my role
from full-time adult psychiatrist with sectoral responsibility
for all age-groups to part-time general psychiatrist and part-
time psychogeriatrician. A 21-bed female long-stay admission
ward was converted into an admission ward with 16 female and
five male beds; and one male and one female long-stay geriatric ward, of 28 and 30 beds respectively, were acquired from
the retiring geriatric physician, in addition to one female
long-stay psychogeriatric ward of 32 beds formerly looked after
by another psychiatrist. With the acquisition of these 90
additional beds, the die was cast for the birth of the Hollymoor Psychogeriatric service.

POLICY

When I became a part-time psychogeriatrician, I relinquished
some of my responsibility for general psychiatry. Even so, it
remained an impossible task at that stage to provide a comprehensive psychogeriatric service for the whole catchment area.
Moreover, the need of the hour seemed to be an organised service for ambulant demented patients. Agreement was reached
with fellow consultants that all demented patients, irrespective of age, would be referred to the consultant in charge of
the psychogeriatric service. By proper channelling of referrals, assessment, organisation of community care, day care
hospital admission and terminal in-patient care, a foundation
was laid for the eventual development of a comprehensive psychogeriatric service (Gaspar, 1980).
    Some referrals for other psychiatric problems in old age

were also accepted irrespective of catchment area. Therefore, from the beginning, the psychogeriatric service handled a growing number of referrals of patients suffering from diseases other than dementia, as it evolved towards a comprehensive service.

STAFF

In addition to the consultant psychogeriatrician, one whole-time clinical assistant (nine sessions per week) and one rotational registrar were appointed to the psychogeriatric team. The hospital-based social work department seconded a social worker and the occupational therapy department appointed a part-time therapist. The director of nursing services brought the four wards under the leadership of a unit nursing officer. In 1976 a community psychiatric nurse was appointed. Thus, doctors, nurses, social worker and occupational therapist formed a psychogeriatric team, and the admission ward became the centre of its activity. The medical secretary came to learn the divisions of responsibility and distribution of cases and to know the people in different agencies, such as old people's homes and day centres, to whom the team related.

GROWTH AND DEVELOPMENT

The outpatient clinic at East Birmingham Hospital provided a vantage point for seeing new and discharged patients with functional illnesses, and for investigating presenile and early old age dementia. In 1983 a psychogeriatric day unit was opened at East Birmingham Hospital, after eight years of planning. Before this the adult psychiatric day unit at Hollymoor Hospital was used for patients suffering functional illnesses in old age. Day places were made available in the admission and long stay wards for the day care of demented patients. Unfortunately, the patients have to travel an average of 28 miles each time they attend for day care. There are now the equivalent of two whole-time community psychiatric nurses working in the team. I have further relinquished my general psychiatric commitments and the unit now provides a comprehensive psychogeriatric service for the Birmingham sector (162,000 population) of the catchment area and a limited service for dementia only in the Solihull sector (108,000 population).

CURRENT OPERATION OF THE SERVICE

Referrals
The main source of referrals is from general practitioners. When referrals come from a social worker, the GP is informed before the patient is seen. Referrals also come from fellow consultants in Hollymoor Hospital and from other hospitals. Referrals are assessed within a week; urgent cases are seen on

the day of referral. Some patients are admitted; for others an opinion is given and for some others responsibility is taken for follow-up care after discharge from hospital. A large number of referred patients live in old people's homes.

Assessment
The aims of assessment are:

1. to establish the presence of dementia;
2. to exclude significant physical problems, especially those causing immobility;
3. to establish that because of behavioural problems or high dependency more than social care is required.

When the referral has been identified as a case of dementia with behavioural problems in an ambulant patient, further assessment is made on the following physical, social and psychological dimensions:

1. How much psychological and neuropsychiatric function is still left.
2. To what degree the patient is beset with physical problems like diabetes, cardiac failure, or respiratory infection which are not causing severe incapacity. Physical illnesses which are within the competence of a general practitioner to treat should be acceptable to a psychogeriatrician.
3. Most important of all is the degree of social support that exists for the key supporter of the patient. As dementia develops, a 'key supporter' emerges for every patient – spouse, daughter, niece or a kindly neighbour who looks after the patient. It is necessary to assess how much practical help and emotional support the key supporter is receiving. The maintenance of the patient at home rests on the goodwill and health of the key supporter. Hence the strategy of supporting the key supporter.
4. To identify the behavioural problems that cause anxiety and annoyance to the relatives. It is one thing to care for a demented patient who is incapable of self-care, but quite a different matter to put up with unwarranted hostile accusations, aggressive outbursts, endless pottering around the house, wandering, being found by the police, or incessant talking and giggling. Some patients become tearful, weepy and depressed. Many relatives would be willing to look after them if only their behaviour was more tolerable. A psychiatrist is able to appreciate that such behaviour results from an interplay of constitutional, dynamic and organic factors and can be alleviated through psychotropic drugs, and tactful handling.

Counselling the relatives in simple ways of handling
the patient is necessary. This is based on the understanding of the emotional reactions of the relative towards the patient, agony over the beloved
one's decline and anger over irascible behaviour.
Enabling relatives to ventilate their feelings over
the inexorable deterioration of the patient is the
essence of supportive psychotherapy. In this way
the initial domiciliary assessment is combined with
therapeutic action.

Outpatients

The author's outpatient clinic has taken on an increasing number of psychogeriatric patients. All demented patients are
assessed at home, but non-urgent functional patients, especially those under 75 years of age, and those who do not suffer
from concurrent physical illnesses, are seen as outpatients.
The outpatient clinic is a suitable place for investigating
patients with suspected dementia for possible remediable causes; and for follow-up of discharged functional patients capable of travelling to the outpatient department. Twenty-
five patients attend for regular lithium check up.

Community Nursing

The bulk of the community care work falls upon the community
psychogeriatric nurse who is the principal supportive psycho-
therapist to the key supporters of the patients, besides providing practical tips and tangible help. Her work with patients suffering from functional illness, and the help she
gives to their supporters, are of equal value.

The Admission Ward

The multi-disciplinary weekly ward round in the admission ward
is the only occasion in the week when all the members of the
team meet together. The activities include teaching in clinical psychiatry, old age psychology and social care and in
tackling administrative problems. The registrar presents the
case of one patient at length for teaching purposes. Members
of the four disciplines bring up their problems. Patients
who have been discharged recently, or a long time previously,
and who have been seen on an after-care visit by one of the
team are mentioned so that other members know what is happen-
ing to a patient whom they have cared for in the ward, and who
is now receiving after-care in the community. The medical
secretary joins this weekly ward round to enjoy a feeling of
team spirit. Not infrequently visitors from the social services department and the occupational therapy department come
to attend the ward round. Medical participation helps to identify and exclude organic cases, as well as patients in an
actively psychotic state. Physical methods of treatment including ECT (Electro Convulsive Therapy) are freely used.

The nurses in the former continuing care wards have undergone a painful readjustment since the unit came into existence. As the long stay chronic schizophrenic patients died, they were replaced by patients suffering from severe dementia who required much more care. The nurses in the admission ward now make a valuable contribution through nursing observation. The shortened version of the Stockton Geriatric Rating Scale for scoring disability level is used by the nurses as a standard procedure for every patient (Gilleard and Pattie, 1977). Among the activities in the admission ward mention must be made of the supportive group therapy (open group) conducted by the occupational therapist. Every six months one of the trainee registrars joins her as co-therapist.

The social worker spends one afternoon each week in the admission ward, enabling patients and relatives to see her easily and to ask for advice and help before discharge. She has advertised in the local press for families to foster patients who express a desire to live with a family rather than alone or in residential accommodation. Two patients have been successfully placed and have survived for more than twelve months. Their progress is monitored through the outpatient clinic.

Education

Hollymoor Hospital has always received final year medical students for clinical attachment and I have always had a medical student attached to my unit. In the past, it was necessary to practice general psychiatry so that the medical student would see the whole spectrum of psychiatric problems and not simply those of old age. However, the wide experience now provided in the unit offers suitable training in many branches of psychiatry and the medical student now spends his time wholly with the psychogeriatric team.

The unit is recognised for training senior registrars in psychiatry. Of the four senior registrars who have passed through the unit, two have become psychogeriatricians. Senior registrars in geriatric medicine have undertaken clinical attachments lasting one month and have found the experience valuable. The psychiatric registrars at Hollymoor Hospital go through a rotational programme and work in each consultant's unit for six months. A longer period of attachment in a psychogeriatric unit is desirable, as it will help doctors to understand the aftercare requirements better, as well as the recurrent nature of depressive breakdowns, the gradual decline among demented patients and the support measures required by the family. The unit is recognised for nurse training by the General Nursing Council. The admission ward and one of the long-stay wards, which is also a second line admission ward, take nursing students. The unit also participates in the training programme for postgraduate students of social work doing an advanced course on Mental Health of the Elderly.

Medical students, registrars, student nurses and trainee occupational therapists go periodically to old people's homes, to specialised residential homes for the elderly mentally infirm, and to local authority day centres to gain knowledge of what the social services offer in the care of the elderly.

RESULTS

In the first three years of the service, between July 1976 and June 1979, 230 referrals for organic mental illnesses were received. The outcome of these referrals is shown schematically in Figure 11.1. Three-quarters of the referred cases were accepted as appropriate to the psychogeriatric service. One-half of these were considered suitable for care at home; and two-thirds of these, or one-third of all appropriately referred patients, remained at home throughout the illness, with support from the community psychiatric nurse, especially in the terminal stages. Of the other one-half of referrals who were admitted to hospital nearly half were able to return home after assessment and treatment.

Figure 11.1: Three years' referrals (July 1976-June 1979.
               N = 230)

1. Outcome of domiciliary assessment by psychiatrist

    1.1   55 patients required social care only; or suffered
          significant physical illnesses (24%)
    1.2   175 patients accepted as psychogeriatric responsi-
          bility (76%)

2. Care of psychogeriatric patients (N = 175)

    2.1   Community care (N = 61; 53%)
          Some patients able to remain at home - with support
          - till death; some admitted to geriatric bed when
          serious physical illness supervened; some subse-
          quently admitted to terminal dementia ward
    2.2   Hospital admission (N = 83; 47%)
          3/8 of admissions returned home after improvement.
          The remainder received continuing hospital care

Since 1979 the work of the unit has steadily expanded, apart from an interruption in 1982 due to industrial action, which prevented the use of available beds. The number of patients suffering organic mental illness admitted remained steady at about one a week. There was a continuing increase in the number of cases of functional illness and in the proportion of all admissions which were for functional illness, as shown in Table 11.1

Table 11.1:   Hollymoor Psychogeriatric Service
Admissions by diagnostic grouping, 1979-82

Year	Number of admissions			Functional as a percentage of all admissions
	Functional	Organic	Total	
1979	37	53	90	41
1980	42	65	107	38
1981	62	60	122	51
1982	54	42	96	56

CONCLUSIONS

The wide scope of activities now conducted by the Hollymoor
Psychogeriatric team is summarised in Figure 11.2. The work
has now been brought under one group whose main orientation is
the care of the elderly psychiatric patients. One consultant,
by taking over primary responsibility for the elderly, has
focused attention on their needs and has enabled staff to
refine their skills and enrich their knowledge. I now find
plenty of job satisfaction and this feeling is shared by all
my team. It is hoped that patients and relatives benefit from
this new method of working.

Figure 11.2: <u>Summary of Work of Hollymoor Psychogeriatric Service</u>

1. <u>Domiciliary Assessment of Demented Patients</u>
    Planned visit and initiating suitable form of care.

2. <u>Outpatient Work</u>
    New patients (functional illness).
    Follow-up of patients discharged from hospital.
    Investigation of presenile and early old age dementia.

3. <u>Day Care</u>
    Mild to moderate cases of organic mental illness.
    Functional illnesses (in some cases ECT given to day
        patients).

4. <u>Community Care</u>
    Dementia of all grades of severity.
    Functional illnesses - some patients who have never been
        to hospital either as outpatient, day-patient or in-
        patient.
    The principal worker is the community psychogeriatric
        nurse, though others play a part.

5. <u>Liaison Work</u>
    Geriatric medical ward.
    Ward referrals from other psychiatric wards.
    Other wards - orthopaedic, surgical, medical, etc.

6. <u>Admission Ward</u>
    Dementia - Holiday relief,
                Investigation and amelioration of symptoms,
                In delirious crisis.
    Functional illness cases.

7. <u>Continuing Care Wards</u>
    Mostly (90%) demented patients and some intractable
        depressives.

8. <u>Advice to General Practitioner in Selected Cases</u>
    Either GP will continue with treatment on his own or
        through members of primary care team.

POSTSCRIPT: THE WIDER CONTEXT

Psychogeriatric services are numerous throughout the United Kingdom with, in 1983, around one-third of all health districts having a designated person responsible for the service. It may be a consultant psychiatrist with exclusive responsibility for meeting the mental health needs of the elderly; or a general adult psychiatrist devoting half or rather more of his time to the psychiatry of old age. Training posts in psychogeriatrics have been established at senior registrar level, which is roughly equivalent to a senior resident or a holder of a fellowship in the United States. These are usually rotational posts giving two years experience at this level of training in adult psychiatry including some of its specialist branches and two years in the psychiatry of old age. These training posts are also available for shorter periods of training for senior registrars who will not necessarily specialise in old age psychiatry, but who will be treating many elderly patients. The Royal College of Psychiatrists has recommended criteria for training posts and for consultant posts.

The Report of the United Kingdom Health Advisory Service, entitled 'The Rising Tide' (1983), defined the requirements for a comprehensive district-based psychogeriatric service. It stressed the need for collaboration between the different branches of the health service and the social services, as well as voluntary organisations, in the planning and establishment of comprehensive programmes. Development has been restricted by national resource problems; but central government and the Regional and District Health Authorities have reiterated their commitment to the expansion of psychogeriatric services as one of the leading priorities for the limited development funds.

The first University chair in the psychiatry of old age was established in 1983 at Guy's Hospital, London; although several years previously the chair of health care of the elderly at Nottingham was filled by a psychogeriatrician.

All new psychogeriatric services have had to struggle with resource problems and with the establishment of good working relationships with colleagues in adult psychiatry, geriatric medicine, general practice, social services and voluntary organisations. Small but distinct advances are being made. An encouraging feature is the support given to relatives through such organisations as the Alzheimer's Disease Society. There have been substantial advances in the academic side with a much better understanding of the psychiatric conditions of old age. The psychiatry of old age is at least beginning to achieve a more sympathetic understanding; and the situation at Hollymoor is typical of what is emerging in other parts of the United Kingdom.

REFERENCES

Bergmann, K. (1979) 'Neurosis and Personality Disorder in Old
    Age' In A. D. Isaacs and F. Post (eds.) Studies in
    Geriatric Psychiatry, Wiley, Chichester
Department of Health and Social Security (1971) 'Hospital
    Services for the Mentally Ill', Circular HM (71) 97,
    HMSO, London
Department of Health and Social Security (1972) 'Services for
    Mental Illness Related to Old Age', Circular HM (72) 71,
    HMSO, London
Fuller, J., Ward, E., Evans, A., Massam, K. and Gardner, A.
    (1979) 'Dementia: Supportive Group for Relatives',
    British Medical Journal, 1, 1684-5
Gaspar, D. (1980) 'Hollymoor Hospital Dementia Service:
    Analysis of Outcome of 230 Consecutive Referrals to a
    Psychiatric Hospital Dementia Service', The Lancet, 1,
    1402-5
Gilleard, C. and Pattie, A. H. (1977) 'Stockton geriatric
    scale. Shortened version with British normative data',
    British Journal of Psychiatry, 131, 90-4
Health Advisory Service (1982) The Rising Tide, NHS Health
    Advisory Service, Sutton
Kay, D. W. K., Beamish, P. and Roth, M. (1964) 'Old Age Mental
    Disorders in Newcastle-upon-Tyne', British Journal of
    Psychiatry, 110, 146-58
Office of Health Economics (1979) Dementia in Old Age, OHE,
    London

Chapter Twelve

A DAY CENTRE FOR THE ELDERLY MENTALLY INFIRM

Mary Keegan

Highbury Day Centre is an experiment in the day care of the elderly mentally infirm. It was established in 1978 under the joint auspicies of the City of Birmingham Social Services Department and the then Birmingham Area Health Authority. The concept was jointly planned, jointly financed and jointly run. It is presented as an example of co-operation between a health authority and a social services department.

In this chapter the background of the scheme will be described, followed by an account of how it was established, how it operates and what it costs. Finally, information will be provided on the evaluation of its effectiveness.

THE BACKGROUND

Table 12.1 gives some simplified figures to demonstrate the need for community support of old people suffering from dementia. The calculations are based on the Newcastle-on-Tyne survey dating from the early 1960s, which estimated that 10 per cent of the population aged 65 and over living at home suffered from significant dementia, one-half of these being severe cases, and that 15 per cent of this population suffered from other mental illness (Kay, Beamish and Roth, 1964). Since then the proportion of the 65 and over population who are very old has risen steeply, and it is among this very old group that dementia is more prevalent, more severe and less well supported.

The table shows that if every geriatric psychogeriatric bed, and residential place in a 'notional' health district was filled with people with dementia to the exclusion of all other categories of patients, there would still be twice as many demented people outside institutions as inside them. In fact only about half of institutional beds house demented patients. At a conservative estimate some 5 per cent of the population aged 65 and over who live at home suffer from significant mental illness and are a source of problems to others. In the average health district, with a population of 250,000 of whom some 14 per cent are aged 65 and over, there must be around 1,750 significantly demented old people at home.

Table 12.1:   Estimate of the care needs of old people
              with mental illness and resources in a 'notional'
              health district

	Basis of Estimate	Source of Estimate	Estimated Number
Population			
Total	Notional		250,000
Number aged 65+	14% of population	(1)	35,000
'Demented' people	10% aged 65+	(2)	3,500
Resources			
Beds - geriatric	10 per 1000 aged 65+	(3)	350
psychogeriatric	3.5 per 1000 aged 65+	(3)	100
residential homes (local authority, private and voluntary)[1]	25 per 1000 aged 65+	(3)	875
Total 'demented'			3,500
Total institutional places			1,325

1. Social Trends, 1984.
2. Kay, Beamish and Roth, 1964.
3. Guidelines quoted in DHSS (1976)

One day centre cannot solve this problem. Of itself it can help
only a fraction of those in need.   It may however be able
to demonstrate ways in which help can be given.   Some other
principles which have been learned from experience of working
at Highbury Day Centre may be put into practice in simpler
ways without replication of all the facilities of the day
centre.
     For example, relatives' support groups, an important
outcome of the Highbury Centre, can be established cheaply in
many localities.

OBJECTIVES

In 1976 a working party was set up, under the chairmanship of
the then community physician for social services of the
Birmingham Area Health Authority. The Committee had representatives of the City of Birmingham Social Services Department,

A Day Centre for the Elderly Mentally Infirm

the geriatric and psychiatric services of South and Central
Birmingham and the department of geriatric medicine of the
University of Birmingham. The group planned the day centre
for the elderly mentally ill with the following objectives:

1.   To provide day care for elderly people suffering
     from mental illness, mainly dementia, who were
     looked after in the community, in the hope of
     improving their physical and mental well being;
2.   To provide relief, guidance, information and
     support to the carers of these old people;
3.   To strengthen links between the psychiatric,
     geriatric and social services;
4.   To act as a focus of education and research in
     the care of the elderly mentally ill.

The working party evolved a brief for the day centre. This was
the basis of a successful submission to the joint consultative
committee and joint funding (2) was obtained with an initial
annual budget of under £30,000 at 1976 prices.

THE BRIEF

Location
Premises were found in an unused part of Highbury Hall, a large
'institutional' type of old persons' home built in the 1930s by
the then Corporation of Birmingham. The institution adjoined
the mansion and parklands of the Chamberlain family home. The
premises comprised two large rooms for the activities of the
'members' as they came to be called; a small combined office,
staff room and kitchen; and toilets. The centre is in a residential area half a mile from shops and buses. Twenty members
can be accommodated daily.

Catchment Area
The geography of Birmingham and its hospitals has defied
attempts to align the catchment areas of psychiatric, geriatric
and social services. However, in four city wards these services overlapped, and these wards were chosen as the catchment
area of the day centre. The population was 160,000 of whom
about 25,000 were aged 65 and over, giving a potential client-
ele of about 1,000. If members attend on average twice a week
for an average period of six months, 100 can attend each year,
i.e. about 10 per cent of those potentially in need.

Community Services
The community services available in the catchment area comprise:

1.   Approximately 75 general practitioners.
2.   One hospital-based community psychiatric nurse for

elderly.
3. Two geriatric health visitors.
4. Two social work area teams.

These were backed by the following institutional resources:

1. One fifteen-bedded ward in a psychiatric hospital.
2. One day hospital for the elderly mentally ill with twelve places.
3. Two hundred and twenty-five hospital beds in departments of geriatric medicine (this is a notional figure for the catchment area population)
4. A day hospital with 50 places.
5. A notional 500 places in residential homes for the elderly.
6. An insignificant number of places in private residential and nursing homes.

The Clients

The clients of the day centre were defined as elderly people suffering from mental illness, mainly but not exclusively dementia, who were being cared for at home with difficulty, but who were not so physically incapacitated, mentally disturbed or socially deprived as to be in need of care in a geriatric, psychiatric or social services residential unit.

Referral Procedure

The original plan envisaged that potential members were to be referred by general practitioners, community psychiatric nurses, health visitors, social workers or hospital doctors. They were to be assessed at home by a doctor who would form part of the Highbury team. His report would be considered by an admission panel, comprising the day centre staff, and consultant advisers from the geriatric, psychiatric and social services, who would decide whether admission to the day centre was appropriate, or whether some alternative placement was preferable. The general practitioner was to be notified of the decision and appropriate action pursued.

The scheme did not work as planned. The first medical officer, himself a general practitioner, was reluctant to pass judgement on the patients of other practitioners. The care staff wished to make their own domiciliary assessments, and attendance of outside consultants at panel meetings proved practically difficult. The system which evolved was that on receipt of a referral the care staff made a home visit and reported their assessment to the general practitioner. They did not accept patients whose behaviour disturbance was so mild that the centre was not necessary; nor those whose disturbance was so severe that they would not have benefited from the centre. Those who appeared to be suitable were brought to the day centre for full evaluation, including a medical

assessment; and, when necessary, further guidance was sought
from the consultant psychiatrists or geriatricians, after the
agreement of the general practitioner had been obtained.

Transport

Transport difficulties had bedevilled the operation of other
day hospitals and day centres. The initial funding included
provision for the purchase of a six-seat vehicle and the
necessary maintenance and replacement costs. The vehicle is
used to collect and return home those members who have no
other means of reaching the club. During the day it is employed on taking members on outings, for example to local
shops and parks.

Staff

The care team was headed by a manager who worked with a
deputy and three care assistants. Allowance was also made for
40 hours of domestic help, 15 hours of secretarial help, a
full-time driver and a medical officer.

Recruitment of the manager proved difficult. Originally
an occupational therapist was sought but no applications were
received. The required professional qualifications were
therefore broadened and appointments were made ad hominem.
The first manager was a kindergarten teacher and her success-
or a psychologist. Both proved highly successful in their
post.

The doctor was a general practitioner with a special
interest in the subject but no additional professional qualifications in geriatric medicine or psychiatry. The medical
officer works closely with the staff, and with the visiting
consultants in geriatric medicine and psychiatry. All new
members have a complete medical examination. The diagnosis
and proposals for treatment are decided in collaboration with
the member's GP and with specialist(s) where appropriate. At
daily senior staff meetings the medical officer monitors the
waiting list, arranges domiciliary visits and participates in
discussions about allocation of places. Each member's GP is
kept informed about changes or progress. The medical officer participates in individual and group therapy and is
available for counselling relatives. She also helps with
staff training, and with maintaining records. The manager,
deputy manager and doctor all devote a lot of time to education, fulfilling many lecturing engagements on the work of the
day centre.

Training

The bulk of staff training takes place in the day centre, but
outside speakers are sometimes invited to staff meetings.
Topics discussed include availability of and eligibility for
state services and cash benefits; the process of human ageing and the nature of physical and mental problems in old age,

the promotion of continence and the management of incontinence; prescribing in old age; confidentiality in professional care and the problems of relatives who care for mentally
infirm old people. Staff members are encouraged to attend
seminars and day release schemes organised locally by the
Social Services Department, the University of Birmingham, Age
Concern and other organisations. Staff turnover has been low,
and morale has remained high. All staff are involved in the
centre's activities and are encouraged to express their views
and ideas, which helps to sustain interest and enthusiasm.

THE PROGRAMME

The day begins with the collection of members from their
homes. The minibus and driver, together with a care assistant, set off at 9 am daily, and collect up to 15 members. For
members who are mentally clear or who have relatives to help
them, this is straightforward. For those who live alone and
are disoriented, the arrival of the minibus driver may be the
first contact they have had with the outside world since their
last attendance at the centre or visit from the home help.
The member may be in a state of undress or in bed; or con-
cocting something suspect on the stove. She is almost invariably unaware that she is to visit the day centre. Patience
and tact are required. The driver and care assistant reassure the member that it is quite in order for her to dress,
leave home, attend the day centre for lunch and return home,
reminding her of pleasant experiences at the centre on her
last visit. The staff ensure that she is appropriately
dressed, check that cookers and fires are turned off, doors
locked and stale food thrown away, and that the member has
her handbag and keys. About one-quarter of members are fetch-
ed by taxi paid for from centre funds, or are brought by
relatives.
     On these daily visits to members' homes an eye is kept
out for signs of neglect: lack of food, strange smells,
accumulating unpaid bills, inappropriate toiletting or hoard-
ing of medicines. The visits also provide an opportunity to
keep in touch with relatives or neighbours.
     At the centre, members meet over the morning cup of tea.
They are encouraged to take their turn in helping to prepare
the tea, even if they need supervision and help from the
staff. Before lunch activities are offered. Creative activities include collage, painting, flower arranging, handi-
crafts and carpentry. Recreational activities include 'keep
fit', skittles, bowls, darts, snooker and, most popular of
all, music, singing and dance. Retention or re-emergence of
skills and even learning new skills is possible. Interaction
is important in stimulating individuals' participation in
activities. Activities of daily living include tea-making,
self-care and attention to personal hygiene. For members who

feel dejected and who no longer take pride in their appearance,
a hair-do, a shave or a bath makes them feel better and pro-
motes confidence. Crosswords, word association games, dominoes and quizzes can help to stimulate mental activity, as also
can group discussions and reminiscing. Outings are an important part of the programme: locally, to the pub, the library,
the shops, the parks and the betting office; also further a-
field, to the country or the sea. When outings are first suggested, there may be little enthusiasm; but almost everyone
enjoys the outing when the time comes, even though many have
forgotten by the following day much of what they experienced.

The daily programme of activities is very flexible, so
that individual needs may be provided for. For example, among
members suffering from depression - sometimes associated with
social isolation - we have had considerable success in encouraging the use of public transport. A staff member accompanies
the old person on the journey by bus between the centre and
home, until the member gains confidence to tackle the journey
alone. The resultant benefits are tremendous: the old person
can now visit her relatives and friends, go to the hairdresser
or to the shops in the city centre.

When no all-day outing is planned, lunch at the centre is
very important. Members are encouraged to take their turn in
helping to set the table for what is, for some, their only
meal of the day. Lunch is delivered from the Social Services
Department cook freeze centre, although on Fridays we order
fish and chips from the local shop. After lunch there is a
quiet period, and members are free to rest or read magazines
and newspapers. Following this, further participation in
fresh activities is encouraged by the staff. Many an afternoon heralds the arrival of visitors, who are invited to join
in whatever events are in progress. Afternoon tea is provided, and again, members help with this. By 4 pm some are
becoming restless or agitated, and anxious to get home. The
minibus driver and escort set out on their return journey.

Attending the centre takes members out of their homes
and offers them a sociable and comfortable environment, and
a welcome rest for the carers. Even a short spell of non-
attendance can have adverse effects on members, as was learned
during the harsh winter of 1981/2, when the centre was forced
to close for a short period. Although staff visited and helped
members at home, there was a marked deterioration in the functioning of even the most able members by the time the centre
re-opened.

Since the centre opened, ways have been developed,through
experience and common-sense, for handling some of the special
problems of elderly mentally infirm people - disorientation in
place and time; anxiety; difficulties in communicating, and
aggressive behaviour.

A Day Centre for the Elderly Mentally Infirm

REALITY ORIENTATION

One of the most disabling features of brain failure is disorientation which, accompanied by poor short-term memory, can lead to a confused and agitated state of mind. Our approach is akin to Reality Orientation (Folsom, 1968). Encouraging orientation in place and time, and recognition of self and others is vital if the member is going to be able to continue living at home. The method is to help the disorientated person re-learn and continually rehearse basic information about time, place and person. The success of this derives from mobilising the member's long-term memory store and gradually, through conversation, leading them on to the realities of the present. Conversations comparing past and present also create occasions conducive to sociability among members: there are many shared memories and experiences. For members who have poor short-term memory and a short span of attention, constant stimulation is needed to maintain interest. Past and present occupations, hobbies and ways of life are all topics for discussion. Staff use many different cues to stimulate reminiscence and conversation: books, pictures, mementoes of both World Wars, film, medals, photographs, antiques, old recipes and remedies, newspaper cuttings, postcards, fabrics and flowers. Memories can be invoked in association with all the senses: smell, taste, hearing and touch. 'Age Concern' have produced a useful film entitled 'Recall', which provoked interesting comments and reactions.

To maximise the effectiveness of this film of reality orientation, the right atmosphere must be established. Members' confidence can be enhanced through friendliness and politeness. It is important to get to know each individual as well as possible, to identify oneself by name when communicating with members and to impart full information in response to worries or queries. If a member is anxious to go home, one way to reassure her might be to tell her 'It is now three o'clock in the afternoon, time for tea. By the time we have cleared away the tea things, it will be almost four o'clock. Then the minibus driver, Colin, will take you home in the minibus. If she cannot remember where she has left her handbag, or whether she has paid her rent, we can usually reassure her by providing the answer. It is then possible to introduce her to some activity or topic of conversation with which she feels comfortable. Knowledge of members' habits and family circumstances enable staff to give correct reassuring advice. It is undesirable, and possibly dangerous, to sustain or encourage delusions.

In our experience, lack of uniform and other signs of authority help to create a pleasant atmosphere. The staff are friendly and capable of using their imagination and initiative. They react calmly to irrational behaviour and respond warmly to periods of lucidity. Their work ensures that the members are more aware of their surroundings and less anxious about their worries.

For effective communication with elderly mentally infirm people, one has to cultivate a special skill for listening and for discriminating between accurate and inaccurate information. If speech continues to be disoriented and deluded one can encourage a more lucid interval by talking about an earlier, happier time in her life. Great value is attached to reminiscing, to learning what were the significant events of past life, what events caused distress, what was valued and what was not valued. These stories can give clues as to what the old person wants for today, as well as promoting feelings of comfort, hope and a sense of achievement and satisfaction.

The staff must appreciate the age difference between themselves and the members and be careful to avoid condescension. Old people have a right not to be patronised as 'old dears'. There have been a great many changes in the spoken English Language over the last 80 years, and we must remember that common expressions of today might not be understood, and some might even offend.

Staff are taught that, when communicating with the hard of hearing, they should face the old person, speak clearly and not too fast. There is no need to shout, as raised voices may cause ridicule from others and embarrassment for the old person. Don't speak with your hand in front of your mouth, or with a cigarette, pipe or pen in it. Avoid jargon or words that might be misunderstood and do not change the subject suddenly. With patience and understanding even those members who are hard of hearing can enjoy a conversation. Management of the aggressive and verbally abusive person requires exceptional skill and patience if violence is to be prevented. The aggression is often a response to something the old person regards as threatening. In their confusion they misinterpret people and things in their environment. There should be no hint of annoyance or reciprocal hostility, since these may be the only signals received by the disturbed old person. Quiet reassurance may give the old person some contact with reality and enable her to be calmed.

MEMBERS' RELATIVES

Relatives are encouraged to participate in the day-to-day running of the centre and to share their problems with staff and with other relatives who are looking after mentally infirm old people. Social events are organised at the centre, to bring together relatives and friends of members who may feel isolated with their problems. These social functions also provide opportunities for relatives to see members enjoying themselves; and to learn from staff and from each other about any particularly successful way of responding to members' disturbed behaviour or difficult habits. Relatives also come to accept

that it is illness which is responsible for the old person's
altered personality and behaviour.

Relatives often continue to offer voluntary help after a
member has moved into an institution or has died. They make
invaluable voluntary helpers, since they have great insight
into the problems of members and of those who look after them
at home.

REFERRALS

Written referrals are accepted from health and social work
professionals in the catchment area. During the period
September 1981 to August 1982, 63 referrals were dealt with,
42 women and 21 men (see Table 12.2) were dealt with. Thirty-
one of these came from social workers, and 17 from community
nurses or health visitors. Eleven were from hospital consultants and three from general practitioners. The diagnosis was
dementia in about two-thirds of referrals, and depression in
about one-quarter. The predominant problems precipitating
referral were high dependency, restlessness, depression,
aggressive behaviour, delirium and wandering. Twenty-six of
the women, almost two-thirds, lived alone, as opposed to seven,
or one-third, of the men.

Table 12.2:   Referrals

Source of referral	Women (42)	Men (21)
Community social worker	17	11
Geriatric health visitor	7	4
Consultant geriatrician	5	4
Consultant psychiatrist	2	
Community psychiatric nurse	6	
Hospital social worker	2	1
Family referral	1	
General practitioner	2	1
Total	42	21

People living alone were usually referred in the hope that
support from the centre would enable them to reamin in their
homes; whereas an important reason for referral of people
living with others was the provision of relief for relatives.
The age distribution of those referred is shown in Table
12.3.

A Day Centre for the Elderly Mentally Infirm

Table 12.3: Age distribution of referrals during the twelve months to August 1982

Age	Women (42)	Men (21)
Less than 60 years	1	
60–69	5	2
70–79	18	11
80–89	15	7
90	2	
Unknown	1	1

The procedure for dealing with a referral has been outlined above. The home visit provides the opportunity for initial assessment of the person's physical and mental state, the home circumstances and problems, their own wishes and those of relatives. It also enables us to describe the service we provide, and give information about other supportive services. Following the home assessment, we extend an invitation to the prospective member and her relatives to visit the centre for tea. This is in order to gain the person's trust, to help her to understand our service and to convey to the relatives that we aim to share care, rather than to take over. Our experience with relatives has been that they are seeking relief and support rather than institutional care. Once a place is offered and accepted, the number of weekly attendances is decided and is reviewed about six weeks after the first attendance and regularly thereafter.

As the centre has only 20 places per day, not all who were referred could be accepted. In the twelve-month period to August 1982, 22 women and eleven men were offered places, just under half who were referred.

Sixteen women and nine men commenced attendance at the centre during the twelve month period up to August 1982. The remaining eight patients did not take up places because of changed needs in the interval since assessment. Fourteen women and six of the men were diagnosed as suffering from brain failure and two women and two men had depression. One man was diagnosed as hypomanic. Their ages ranged from 60 years to over 90 years old. Ten of the women and two of the men were living alone. Fifteen people were offered one day's attendance per week, seven were offered two days and three three days or more. The majority was assessed within four weeks of referral, and more than two-thirds had begun attending the centre within six weeks. Very few new members presented with previously undiagnosed medical problems, although a number suffered from hypertension, epilepsy, carcinoma of the breast, iron deficiency, folate deficiency and vitamin B12 deficiency; and there was some incidence of unresolved problems with bowels and feet. Thirteen of those with brain failure were not known to suffer from any other illness.

At the end of the year up to August 1982, sixteen of the 20 people with brain failure were still attending, four of them needing extra attendances. Two of them had died, one refused to attend and one had been admitted to residential care. Three of the four suffering from depression had improved.

Of the sixty-three people referred to the centre during the twelve month period, 30 were not offered places. The reasons for this are shown below.

Table 12.4:

Reasons for not offering a place	Women (20)	Men (10)
Residential accommodation preferred	2	3
Other day care more appropriate	8	1
Died prior to assessment		1
Admitted to geriatric ward		1
Admitted to psychiatric ward	2	1
Not in catchment area	2	2
Too immobile		1
Did not wish to attend	5	
Other	1	

PATTERNS OF ATTENDANCE AT THE CENTRE

Although at the outset we envisaged that some members could be discharged from the centre as their level of functioning improved, this was possible for only a minority. Two women and two men were discharged during the year up to August 1982. One of these had improved, one refused to attend, one was too disruptive, and one was transferred to non-specialist day care. These discharges created six places per week.

When members make some progress, the number of days' attendance may be reduced. Ten places per week become available through reducing attendance, but existing members often require additional support through more frequent attendance. In general, our policy is to offer some support, even if this is minimal, to the greatest possible number of members and their carers. The bulk of turnover resulted from members' decline or admission to permanent care. Six members were admitted, creating eleven places per week, and eight members died, creating twelve places.

To illustrate patterns of attendance, I have taken figures for one week, chosen at random. During the week ending 19 June 1982, 42 members attended the centre. Six attended on all five days; four members on four days; eight members on three days; twelve members on two days and twelve attended on just one day. Fifteen members had been attending the centre for more than two years; 16 had been attending for between six months and two years and eleven had joined the centre less than six months before.

Table 12.5: Numbers of places created during 12 months to August 1982 (Total No. places per week: 100)

Reason	No. of places created	
	Female	Male
Permanent care	11	2
Death	5	12
Discharge	3	3
Reduced attendance	6	4
Total	25*	21*

*46% turnover of places during the year.

PROBLEMS AND POTENTIAL PROBLEMS

There are four major issues of concern. First, our main frustration is the shortage of resources for elderly mentally infirm people and their lay carers. While the geriatric, psychiatric and residential services collaborate with the centre staff in discussing the needs of members, they are rarely able to offer anything other than short-term relief admission even where all agree that more support is needed. Relatives are often driven close to breaking point while waiting for the offer of institutional care. Officers in charge of residential homes believe that their staffing levels are too low to enable them to admit elderly mentally infirm people. Many of them also estimate that up to half their existing residents suffer some degree of mental infirmity. Improved staff training and higher staff: resident ratios are both urgently needed (see Chapter Thirteen).
    Second, a common assumption is that care and control of elderly mentally infirm people is very difficult. However, our experience is that if constraints on members' behaviour are kept to a minimum and opportunities for enjoyable activities are maximised, these people respond well and can be particularly rewarding to work with. Administering medication presents no difficulties, since few members take medicine.
    Third, relatives looking after elderly mentally infirm people may sometimes appear to be very demanding. However, their demands are seldom to do with seeking to relinquish

their caring roles, but rather for a sympathetic listener who
may have practical suggestions to offer when it comes to coping with day-to-day problems and frustrations. Relatives can
telephone the day centre any time during the working day, and
staff always offer support.

The fourth area of difficulty sometimes arises in relationships with members' general practitioners. In most cases,
GPs work very closely with the medical officer and staff team
in planning and reviewing members' care. But sometimes, GPs
appear to attach low priority to the needs of their elderly
mentally infirm patients, and seek to place responsibility for
provision of formal care on the day centre. Not all GPs seem
to provide positive or preventative care for elderly mentally
infirm patients.

EVALUATION

Quantitative data about the work of the centre, in terms of
numbers of referrals, places offered, the members who attend
and the patterns of attendance has been kept since the service was set up. This data, some of which has been presented
above, suggests that we are providing a service for a group
of people for whom sorely needed services have previously
been lacking. As such, if it were possible to make any financial assessment of our service, it would doubtless suggest
that the service represents an extra cost to the public purse
rather than offering any saving (3).

Such evaluation as can be offered relates to quality of
life. We formed the impression that attendance at the centre
perhaps helped some members to remain in their own homes for
longer than might otherwise have been the case. For example,
a woman with a history of psychiatric hospital admissions
over 40 years was not once readmitted during the two-and-a-
half years she attended the centre prior to her death, despite
the fact that her symptoms showed little improvement.

Members enjoy coming to the centre and welcome the companionship. Confidence and independence are increased through
participation in activities they enjoy, in the day-to-day running of the centre and in the rediscovery and recounting of
forgotten tales of past times to younger people. Regaining
the confidence to use public transport has been a great boon
to withdrawn and depressed members. That so many relatives
of deceased members continue to support the centre as voluntary helpers suggest they appreciated the help that day care
at the centre afforded them. They often say that this support
helped to improve severely strained family relationships.

Much of the good work done at the centre is attributable
to the attitude and commitment of the staff team. Improvement
or change in members brings its own reward, and the low turnover among staff facilitates continuity, and indicates that
staff satisfaction is high. The centre has come to be viewed

as a centre of excellence in caring for elderly mentally infirm people, and many professionals and others involved in this field visit Highbury to learn about our work.

POSTSCRIPT

The shortfall in services for elderly mentally infirm people and their lay carers is now widely acknowledged. In other parts of the country, awareness of this vast area of unmet need is stimulating developments akin to that described in this chapter. Collaboration between the health and social services and joint funding is a feature of some; for example two schemes in Buckinghamshire, and a new service in Westminster. The Buckinghamshire schemes rely mainly on volunteers; day centres elsewhere are usually run by teams of paid workers, for example Southwark. Goldberg and Connelly (1982) summarise two evaluative studies (4). One of these is of a Buckinghamshire centre and shows that relatives greatly valued the relief the centre afforded them, and the mentally infirm members of the scheme appeared to be happier in the eyes of both relatives and volunteers at the centre. This is in accord with the experience at Highbury, and reinforces the arguments from demographic imperatives for developing and evaluating further facilities of this type.

NOTES

1. Johnson (1983) quotes official data from 1980 which shows that about 62 per cent of residential places were provided by local authorities; the remainder were in private and voluntary homes.

2. See Chapter Two, p.14 for an explanation of the Joint Funding Scheme.

3. If the policy option of increasing day care provision as an alternative to institutional care was pursued, then we can speculate that the centre would emerge as highly cost effective.

4. Chisholm, L. and Fletcher, P. (1979) 'The Park Club: A study of a club run by voluntary effort to help support confused elderly people and their families'; Buckinghamshire Social Services Department. Mendel, J. (1979) 'Confusion unconfounded', Community Care, 16 August. Mendel, J. (1979) 'Report to Family and Community Services', Sheffield Social Services Department, on MIND's Woodhouse Project; unpublished.

The views expressed in this chapter are personal and do not necessarily represent the official position of the Social Services Department.

REFERENCES

Department of Health and Social Security (1976) Priorities for
    health and personal social services, HMSO, London
Folsom, J. (1968) 'Reality orientation for the elderly mentally
    infirm patient', Journal of Geriatric Psychiatry, 1:
    291-307
Goldberg, E. and Connelly, N. (1982) The effectiveness of
    social care for the elderly. Heinemann Educational Books,
    London
Johnson, M. (1983) 'Private lives', Health and Social Services
    Journal, 28 July, pp. 901-3
Kay, D., Beamish, B. and Roth, M. (1964) 'Old age mental
    disorders in Newcastle-upon-Tyne'; British Journal of
    Psychiatry, 110: 146-58
Social Trends 1984 (1983), 14, HMSO, London

Chapter Thirteen

RESIDENTIAL HOME FOR THE ELDERLY MENTALLY INFIRM

Dorothy Pettitt

HOMES FOR THE ELDERLY - THE BACKGROUND

The provision of homes for the elderly by local authorities
stems from the 1948 National Assistance Act, which was directed towards elimination of the dreaded workhouses. Under Part
III of that Act, local authorities, through their welfare
departments, (now incorporated into Social Services Departments) have the 'Duty to provide accommodation for those who
by reason of age or infirmity are in need of care and attention not otherwise available'. (Section 21, para 5) From
the 1950s onwards, Birmingham, along with other authorities,
embarked on a programme of building homes for the elderly which
provided a high standard of comfort and personal care on hotel
lines. A large number of elderly people were admitted because
they were homeless or lonely rather than because they were
physically or mentally in need of care. Poor mobility, incontinence and mental infirmity were rare characteristics of
residents in those early years.
      The policy at that time was one of providing one type of
home for all elderly people in need of care under the terms of
the Act, whatever their disabilities or social background. Any
suggestion of segregation was not intended by the legislation
and was not acceptable if authorities were to show equal respect and regard for each individual. It was reasonable to
uphold this policy because a high proportion of residents was
ambulant, continent, mentally stable and capable of self-care.
Any deterioration, mentally or physically, resulted in transfer to hospital. Long-stay beds in hospital were available,
though usually on an 'exchange' basis, that is, an exchange
was arranged between a patient requiring a place in a home and
a resident requiring a hospital bed.

REASONS FOR CHANGE IN POLICY

Since the early 1970s this situation has gradually changed for
a number of reasons. First, there has been an upward trend in

both the numbers and the proportion of elderly people in the
population. Secondly, consultant geriatricians have changed
to a dynamic policy of minimising the number of long-term elderly patients; aiming to treat, to improve mobility and to
encourage self-care. As long-term beds have been reduced,
many have been brought into use as short-term relief beds,
providing respite for carers, be it family or good neighbours.
Allied to this was the dislike of health authority and social
services staff for the 'exchange' system and its implied dis-
regard for the individual. Thirdly, there has been a substantial increase in the availability of domiciliary services in
Birmingham. The social services department provides meals for
seven days a week if needed and, in the short-term, a home
help can be provided each day (see Chapter Five).

Thus, the capacity and infirmity of residents have been
influenced on two counts: the more able elderly people are
staying in their own homes rather than entering a residential
home, while hospitals expect a more dependent group of elderly
people to be cared for in these same homes.

In the 1970s the increasing level of infirmity of residents and the growing number who were mentally infirm caused
Birmingham Social Services Committee to question its policy
of providing general purpose homes for all categories of residents. On the whole mentally alert residents lived in harmony
with the mildly confused and would willingly help and befriend
those who were somewhat disorientated in time and place. However, any greater degree of disturbed behaviour - such as
wandering into others' bedrooms, nocturnal wandering, collecting other residents' possessions or showing extreme agitation
- soon caused distress to mentally alert residents.

During the years 1970 to 1976 Birmingham opened ten new
homes for the elderly, each having 60 places. In 1976 a 30-
place home was planned as part of the social services department's capital building programme, and it was proposed that
this smaller home should be designated specifically for elderly mentally infirm clients and that the department should invite the psychiatric and geriatric services to share in a
joint project designed to help the City plan its care of elderly mentally infirm people. Before describing this project and
its outcome, it is of interest to consider the functions of
homes and hospitals in the care of the elderly as set out by
the Ministry of Health in the 1960s.

FUNCTIONS OF HOMES AND GERIATRIC HOSPITALS

The categories of elderly people who should be cared for by
local authorities and in hospital were defined in a Ministry
of Health Circular (No. 77, 1965). In terms of physical infirmity, local authorities were to care for those who, although not capable of carrying out daily living tasks independ-
ently, could get about with the help of aids. Hospitals were

to care for people with long-term illnesses requiring continuous medical or nursing care and for those who were barely mobile and confined to bed or chair. The guidelines also suggested that some incontinent people could have been cared for
in homes, but people with intractable incontinence combined
with other disabilities if untreatable, were defined as needing hospital care.

So far as mental infirmity was concerned homes were to
care for 'people with temporary or continuing confusion of mind
but who do not need psychiatric nursing care',(para 5 (iii))
while hospitals were to care for those suffering from confusion
of mind or mental disorder who could not suitably live in their
own homes or in a residential home.

In subsequent memoranda (for example DHSS, 1972) DHSS
have restated these guidelines,but precise definitions of the
various categories remain lacking. Thus the relative responsibilities of community health and social services, residential
homes, and hospitals — including psychiatric hospitals — remains in part a matter for local negotiation. This is not entirely satisfactory,given that health and social service professionals may have conflicting perspectives on problems, like
mental infirmity. Further, the physical and mental state of
elderly people may not remain static, yet the DHSS Circulars
do not address questions of how best to respond to changes. We
shall return to this question of the functions of homes and
hospitals in the light of the experience of the project.

THE PROJECT — HOME FOR THE ELDERLY MENTALLY INFIRM

The 30-place, single storey home — named 'Woodside' is situated in the southern half of Birmingham. The area is served
by two social services districts and two health districts, and
is within the catchment area of a psychiatric hospital and a
geriatric hospital. The population of these two districts is
469,000, with 69,000 people aged 65 years and over. The
primary aim was to provide the opportunity for social and
medical assessment of elderly mentally infirm people who were
being referred to social work offices as requiring a residential place, and to plan their future care. The hospitals were
approached through the Area community physician. The consultant geriatricians were keen to co-operate, were prepared to
provide domiciliary assessments for applicants and to name a
member of their team to share in admissions conferences.
There is no psychogeriatrician on the establishment of the
psychiatric hospital but a consultant psychiatrist agreed to
support the project. A general practitioner with a special
interest in mental disorder was appointed to provide primary
care to those residents who wished to register with him. A
steering group was formed, consisting of a geriatrician, psychiatrist, home doctor and officer in change; under the
chairmanship of the social services district Manager.

Elderly people considered for admission were disorientated, confused, agitated, depressed or suffering from mild
chronic psychiatric disorders. It was recognised that people
with mental disorders might also suffer from incontinence and
physical infirmities. The latter problems were not regarded
as a prime reason for admission nor did they preclude admission.

During the planning stage much thought was given to the
style of care which was hoped for. Homes for the elderly,
whilst providing satisfactory standards of physical care, can
easily develop the damaging traits of institutionalisation
vividly described in Erving Goffman's **Asylums**. The predominance of rules and routines, and the denial of self-determination can result in dependency, apathy and loss of identity.
Residential work is part of social work and must be based on
the social work principles of respect for the dignity and
worth of the individual, the right to self-determination, the
right to one's own individuality and the opportunity to develop potential. These principles required particularly strong
emphasis in Woodside's regime, since the practice and organisation of residential care too often features apparent dis-
regard for the rights of people suffering mental infirmity.

It was envisaged that the assessment period would result
in one of the following outcomes:

1. To remain at Woodside on a long-term basis;
2. to transfer to a general purpose home for the
   elderly;
3. to transfer to hospital - geriatric or psychiatric -
   on a short or long-term basis;
4. to return home.

Procedures for Admission and Assessment

Before explaining the procedures adopted at Woodside , it is
of interest to explain the admission procedure used for other
homes for the elderly. Birmingham with its one million population had approximately 2600 places in 50 homes for the elderly run by the social services department. The allocation
of places in homes was administered by one central placements
section. The staff of the section received applications from
social workers, and acted as intermediaries between social
workers and officers in charge of homes in deciding the
allocation of places. The applicant visited the home and the
officer in charge visited the client before the final decision was made. No case conferences or allocations meetings
were held as a general rule.

The procedure established for Woodside broke new
ground. Referrals from social workers - field or hospital -
are passed directly to the home and the geriatrician, psychiatrist and staff of home carry out a domiciliary assessment.
A fortnightly meeting to decide on admissions includes the

geriatrician, psychiatrist and social worker for the applicant.
At this meeting the client's suitability for Woodside is debated. The consultants might diagnose a treatable condition;
or the social worker might offer support services to client
and relatives which would allow the person to stay at home.
Thus the multi-disciplinary assessment and the subsequent discussion,selects for Woodside those people who are in the
early stages of dementia, or suffering a mild psychotic illness, and seeks out the best alternative for those who are not
selected for admission. Following admission the assessment
and monitoring of residents is continuous, each resident being
allocated to a member of staff who becomes the 'attached'
worker.

The Staff at Woodside
At its inception, Woodside was given the following assignment
of staff:

Post	Hours per week	Salary (1983 value) per annum
Officer in Charge	40	£9231-£10,071
Deputy Officer	40	£7545-£ 8949
Third Officer	40	£6873-£ 8055
Care Assistant	410	£4643
Domestic Assistant	120	£4081
Cook	60	£4741
Launderer	20	£4546

The officer in charge was a state registered nurse who had
several years of experience in charge of a general purpose
home for the elderly, but who had previously been a fostering
and adoption officer with a voluntary organisation. She had
geriatric and psychiatric nursing experience in hospitals, and
had worked as a health visitor. Although she was not qualified in social work she had proven management and innovatory
skills.
    None of the other staff held any professional qualifi-
cations, but many had experience in working with the elderly.
The care staff were recruited on an hourly paid manual grade.
The group appointed were mixed; some young, some middle-aged
and of either sex. Additionally, the team leader, i.e. the
supervisor of the officer in charge, was a registered mental
nurse; and this area of knowledge and training proved invaluable in supporting and advising the staff of the home.
The appropriateness of staffing levels will be discussed
later.

Residential Home for the Elderly Mentally Infirm

The Programme at Woodside

The care provided is based on the principle that respect and regard for the individual is paramount. This principle is especially important in the care of elderly mentally infirm people. Rules and routines are kept to a minimum, and each individual is encouraged to maintain his capacity for self care.

Within this framework, the attached worker takes the central role in the continuing assessment and care of his residents. Charts are kept to record sleep patterns and incontinence. Residents are free to get up and go to bed when they wish. Periodic records are made of residents' abilities to carry out simple activities of daily living. Reality orientation is used to help orientate residents in time, place and personal identity. Residents are free to share in domestic work, e.g. washing up, setting tables, and making beds.

Staff are encouraged to spend time with residents: talking, reminiscing, sharing activities with the residents and taking them out. It has become the practice to have music every evening, and residents gather together happily. A drink is provided and residents go contentedly to bed. Relatives are encouraged to call in at any time, but in particular they find the evening social gathering an occasion in which they can easily share.

The GP attached to the home works closely with the staff in monitoring the effects of drugs and, in consultation with the psychiatrist, he reduces medication where possible. The officer in charge welcomes the support of the community nurse who gives a service to the residents and advice to the staff. Regular case reviews are held and include the attached worker, resident, relatives and social worker.

In addition to the fortnightly allocation meetings, a Steering Group meets twice yearly to monitor the achievements of the home. The Steering Group, chaired by the District Manager (Social Services), includes the home GP, geriatrician, psychiatrist, placement officer and senior staff of the home.

RESULTS AND FUTURE PLANNING

The figures of referrals and admissions for the first four years are as follows:

Residential Home for the Elderly Mentally Infirm

Table 13.1:   Referrals and Admissions

	1978	1979	1980	1981
Total referrals	94	80	133	84
No. admitted from hospital	12	6	8	2
own home	10	9	15	15
Part III	7	7	2	2
Total	29	22	25	19

At the start of the project it was decided that 20 of the 30
places should be used for assessment and ten for long-stay
care.   All admissions in the first instance were of people
whose behaviour was not acceptable in general purpose homes,
but who had not yet reached an intractable condition;   and
were still capable of some degree of self care, and thus amenable to help by the assessment and review process.   Those
who could not return home or transfer to an ordinary home remained as long-stay residents.   At the end of the first year
the home had 15 residents requiring long-term care.   At the
end of the second year this number had risen to 23.   By the
end of the third year (October 1980) it was decided to change
two assessment places to rota care places.   Thus the division
of places became 20 for long-stay care, eight for assessment
and two for rota care;   and has remained so until now.
      The increase in long-term places obviously reduced the
number of people who could be admitted.   Referrals remained
high.   The pre-admission assessment procedure continued: on
the basis of the home assessment and a case conference, the
geriatrician and social work staff jointly agreed the needs
of the elderly person.   A breakdown of 160 referrals in
1981/82 divided the assessment as follows:

      53 - more appropriate for general purpose home if had
           to leave own home;
       8 - required hospital care;
      28 - with short-stay in Woodside could stay at home;
      45 - needed long-stay care;
      26 - died or the case was withdrawn.

All those judged to need a specialist EMI (elderly mentally
infirm) unit or a general purpose home benefited from a full
assessment, but unfortunately appropriate places were not
available.   A small minority of assessed patients required
hospital care.

Long-stay Care
At the end of the first year Woodside had 15 residents

requiring long-stay care in a home for the elderly mentally infirm. These residents had responded to care and treatment and
had improved in a variety of ways. For example, the drug regime of eight residents was corrected or discontinued; ten
residents showed improvement in level of communication; 13
showed physical improvement such as weight gain or greater mobility; and 15 responded to stimulation where lethargy and
self neglect has been apparent on admission. Although this
group could not live in a general home for the elderly without
causing distress to mentally alert residents, they were responding to the homely free and easy environment at Woodside,
and none were considered for transfer to a psychiatric hospital. Many of these residents were able to participate in their
own care, responded to reality orientation techniques and enjoyed musical evenings and outings.

By October 1979, when the number of people requiring care
had increased, the staff began to report deterioration in many
residents who were in their second year in the home. Collecting, wandering, and removing clothes were becoming more common
and the effectiveness of reality orientation and social activities was reduced. However, the staff continued to gather
residents together each night for music and a drink to provide
a happy and harmonious end to the day. The average length of
stay is now three years for those who require continuing care
in an EMI home.

Rota Care and other Support for Carers

Clients who returned home after assessment were very dependent
on relatives or neighbours. The opportunity for a client to
stay at Woodside several times a year meant that carers were
provided with constructive help and were able to continue to
give support. A few of these people receiving short-term care
also received day care at a day centre for the elderly mentally
infirm (see Chapter Twelve); and the staff of the two units
worked together to maintain moderately demented clients in
their own homes. Woodside also offered support to relatives
by taking care of an elderly person for an evening or a day in
order to give relatives the opportunity to go out.

Admission to Hospital

A consultant geriatrician has taken a full share in the work
of Woodside; providing assessment and medical examination and
attending allocation and steering group meetings. The input
from the two psychiatrists has been less consistent; but for
a twelve-month period a registrar from the psychiatric hospital gave an excellent service and took a regular part in initial assessments and in monitoring the progress of residents.
Neither geriatricians nor psychiatrists have been eager to
take into hospital those few residents who deteriorate to such
a degree that they need hospital care. It is for the doctors
to say why it is so difficult. It would appear from the

number of hospital beds in Birmingham that we are not without
the resources. When a resident becomes doubly incontinent and
bedfast, or so disturbed as to be a danger to themselves and
others even in a relaxed and free environment, then residential homes cannot provide the care and nursing that is necessary.

ADMISSION TO OTHER HOMES

When the Woodside project was well in progress it became clear
that long-stay care was possible in social services homes for
those elderly with moderate and severe degrees of dementia,
provided that certain conditions were met. Clear objectives
must be set for the unit; staff levels must be high; there
must be good leadership and medical support from psychiatrists
and geriatricians.
    Since 1977 Birmingham social services department has in-
creased its specialist places for the elderly mentally infirm.
Including the 30 places at Woodside there are now 104 places.
There is a joint-funded 50-place home built on a four-unit
plan allowing residents to live in groups of twelve or 13 (1);
and there are two other 50-place homes, each having one
twelve-bedded unit for the elderly mentally infirm. Our progress in providing special units for the elderly mentally infirm has been slow. Birmingham now has 2554 places in homes
for the elderly. The urgent need is to increase the number of
long-stay places for the moderately or severely demented to at
least 25 per cent of this total. Those suffering from memory
loss and mild confusion will continue to live in general purpose units with those who have physical infirmities but who
are mentally alert. However, if the Government objective,
stated in Care in the Community (DHSS, 1981),   to support
elderly people in the community, is rigorously pursued, progressively fewer physically infirm people will be admitted to
homes. The suggested figure of 25 per cent should be considered as provisional, and be subject to continual review.
    The role of Woodside as an assessment unit has proved
successful and needs to continue, (referrals have never
slackened) but the work has been constrained by the lack of
places in other homes to which to transfer long-stay residents
requiring a special unit.

CHARACTERISTICS OF RESIDENTS

Earlier, the Government guidelines on the different functions
of homes and hospitals were set out. It is of interest to
consider the results of two studies designed to measure the
characteristics of residents in homes for the elderly.
Bowling and Bleathman (1982) studied 485 residents in 36 homes
in London Boroughs. Thirty-five per cent were incontinent of
urine; 18 per cent were incontinent of faeces; 45 per cent

needed help with dressing and 30 per cent needed help in getting to the toilet. Using the Crichton Royal Behavioural
Rating Scale (Wilkin and Jolley, 1979) to assess mental functioning, they found that 52 per cent were lucid, 13 per cent
were 'marginal', 16 per cent were moderately confused and 19
per cent were severely confused. A national survey has been
carried out by a team from Kent University, but at the time
of writing the findings are not yet published. Of 2378 residents in homes in Birmingham, 11 per cent were incontinent
of urine; 1 per cent were incontinent of faeces; 12 per
cent were doubly incontinent; 28 per cent needed help with
dressing and 18 per cent needed help getting to the toilet.
Thirty-eight per cent were mentally alert; 39 per cent had
some degree of mental impairment, and 21 per cent had severe
confusion, including deterioration of personality or habits.

The findings from Woodside in this same survey showed
that 4 per cent of residents were incontinent of urine; 4
per cent incontinent of faeces; 34 per cent were doubly
incontinent; 93 per cent needed help with dressing and 93
per cent needed help in getting to the toilet. Twenty per
cent of the residents had a mild degree of mental impairment;
and 80 per cent had severe confusion including deterioration
of personality or habits.

In considering the results of any survey of resident
characteristics, it must be remembered that categorisations
result from human judgements and are partially subjective.
Further, categorisations of residents do not reveal anything
about the style of care. It is possible that confusion and
incontinence are precipitated by the total care routines that
are practised in many homes. New residents very quickly imi-
tate the habits of established residents. Despite these
caveats, the figures confirm that Woodside has received the
group for whom it was intended. The London survey indicates
that these homes are caring for a more physically dependent
group than the Birmingham homes, but the degree of mental
infirmity is similar.

STAFF GRADES AND NUMBERS

The care staff are employed on manual hourly paid grades
with only three senior posts on officer grades. If we are to
attract new entrants looking for a career, we need to raise
the status of care posts to that of officer grades. This is
accepted in child care establishments, and it is hard to understand why homes for adults should be staffed differently.

An issue which is of greater importance is that of staffing levels. In Birmingham homes, day time care staff/resi-
dent ratios have on average been one staff : 20 residents in
practice. The original care staff ratios at Woodside were
only a slight improvement on this; but the officers argued
strongly for an increase. The Social Services Committee

approved the necessary finance, and after 18 months Woodside had a day time ratio of one staff : ten residents in
practice.

If homes are to provide enlightened care, make assessments
which may prevent long-term institutional care, on those who
are physically or mentally infirm, even this improved ratio
is not high enough. However, if we could achieve this improved staffing level in all homes, their staffs would be willing to care for the more dependent residents. The main
problem that Woodside has experienced is the unavailability
of places in other homes for those residents requiring long-
stay care. Without an improved staff/resident ratio in all
homes this problem will persist.

It is compounded by the division of homes for adults
into two categories. In the first category, home staff have
a higher rate of pay than in the second category, on the
assumption that residents in the latter require less care.
This division may have had meaning in the 1950s but not now.
All homes should be changed to the first category. Some
authorities have done this but Birmingham still designates
the majority of its homes as of the second category. The
Social Services Committee is however, now pursuing a policy
of changing the homes built in the 1950s and 1960s into a
group living design. As homes are re-planned, consideration
is being given to both improving staff ratios and changing
the staff grades to the higher category.

SUMMARY AND CONCLUSIONS

In 1976, Birmingham social services department planned a 30-
place home for the elderly mentally infirm. The home was not
joint-funded; but social services asked the geriatric and
psychiatric services to share in a joint project designed to
provide a full medical and social assessment for elderly
mentally infirm people referred by social workers for Part
III accommodation.

Referrals far exceeded available places. Full assessment identified clients' needs and suggested the best possible
plans for their care. Woodside provided a free and homely
environment,with rules and routines kept to a minimum. Care
staff were allocated to specific residents and contributed to
regular case reviews. Reality orientation, incontinence training, activities and entertainment were built into the pattern
of care. Support from geriatricians was constructive and
consistent, but psychiatric support was patchy. Referrals from
hospital and transfers out to hospital were largely with the
geriatric hospital.

The project did not provide an easy answer to the question of segregation or integration of residents suffering from
mental infirmity. The policy that homes provide care for the
elderly whatever their disabilities is generally accepted as

including those with mild confusion or behavioural disorders.
For those with moderate to severe dementia, Woodside has shown
that enlightened care can be provided in a home. However, those
who came in with milder symptoms quickly deteriorated to the
level of those in a more advanced stage of dementia. After the
first year the inability to segregate those coming in for
assessment from the long-stay residents, created problems. The
three homes opened after Woodside are 50-place homes built on
a group-living plan with four groups of twelve or 13 residents.
It would seem that the best plan is to have one or two units
for the elderly mentally infirm, with the other units providing
for the mentally able. Enlightened care can improve the life
style of the elderly mentally infirm but cannot prevent deterioration. Group living allows partial segregation: 'like'
elderly live in a small group, but the groups come together
for activities. Relatives want the elderly mentally infirm to
live in a genuinely caring environment, and are not happy
about their being with those who are 'worse'. Thus, on the
whole, relatives support the division into smaller groups
according to degrees of infirmity.

Woodside encountered the perennial problem of assessment
places becoming long-term, because there were few places elsewhere for long-term care. More homes in the City require an
improved staff ratio, but this would mean doubling the hours
allocated to each home. When this can be combined with re-
grading homes to the higher category, each home can play its
part in providing care for the very infirm. As psychogeriatric
services are improved and as the social services department
pursues its policy of offering more places in homes to the
moderately and severely mentally infirm elderly, Birmingham
will be better equipped to provide for its increasing
frail elderly population.

POSTSCRIPT

Social services departments in other parts of the country
have established specialist homes for elderly mentally infirm
residents. In Newcastle, for example, with a total population
of 300,000, there are now five 40-place homes for this special
group. Those involved with the service report excellent
working relationships with and support from that city's
psychiatric services.

The question of whether mentally infirm residents should
be segregated from the mentally lucid continues to be debated.
Some, for example Meacher (1972) consider that segregation
can too easily result in 'ghettoes' for the mentally infirm
elderly. Evans, Hughes, Wilkin and Jolley (1981) report an
evaluation study of six residential homes, in which they analyse the implications for staff and residents of mixing or
segregating people with differing levels of mental and physical
incapacity. Their finding led them to conclude that there were

advantages for all concerned in integrating not more than 30
per cent of confused residents into the population of old
people's homes. Goldberg and Connelly (1982) consider this
study to be the best yet available, but caution that the conclusions need to be further tested in practice.

There may be a range of possible solutions to local problems of how best to cater for the needs of elderly mentally
infirm people. The specialist home, like the one described
in this chapter, may well offer an invaluable resource for the
elderly mentally infirm and their carers.

NOTES

1. See Chapter Two, p.14 for an explanation of the
Joint Funding scheme.

The views expressed in this chapter are those of the
author, and do not necessarily represent the official position
of the Social Services Department.

REFERENCES

Bowling, A. and Bleathman, C. (1982) 'Beware of the nurses',
    Nursing Mirror, 29 September, pp. 54-8
Department of Health and Social Security (1972) 'Services for
    mental illness related to old age', Circular HM(72)71,
    HMSO, London
Department of Health and Social Security (1981) Care in the
    Community, HMSO, London
Evans, G., Hughes, B. and Wilkin, D. with Jolley, D. (1981)
    The management of mental and physical impairment in non-
    specialist residential homes for the elderly. Research
    Report No. 4, Research Section, University Hospital of
    South Manchester Psychogeriatric Unit, Manchester
Goffman, E. (1961) Asylums, Anchor Books, New York
Goldberg, A. and Connelly, N. (1982) The effectiveness of
    social care for the elderly, Policy Studies Institute,
    London
Meacher, M. (1972) Taken for a ride, Longman, London
Ministry of Health (1965) 'Care of the elderly in hospitals
    and residential homes', Circular HM(65)77, Ministry
    of Health, London
Wilkin, D. and Jolley, D. (1979) Behavioural problems among
    old people in geriatric wards, psychogeriatric wards and
    residential homes 1976-78. Research Report No. 1,
    Research Section, University Hospital of South
    Manchester Psychogeriatric Unit, Manchester

Chapter Fourteen

DOMICILIARY CARE OF THE TERMINALLY ILL

Dewi Rees

'To an increasing extent people now die in hospitals and not
in their homes. The reason for this is usually social and not
medical. The concept that "they look after him better in hospital" is often true only to the extent that it simplifies
the situation for the doctors and nurses, and relieves the relatives of an important responsibility. Often in fact, the
dying person is better cared for at home than in hospital. The
direct care by people of their dying relatives is a considerable help in preparing them for the subsequent bereavement.
This care requires considerable patience. Often it entails
sleepless nights, anxiety and moments of anguish, but the continuity of contact and the realisation that one is caring for
one's own make the effort worthwhile. Many people whose relatives have died in hospital have told me that they would have
preferred them to die at home. No relative of a person who
died at home has told me that they would have preferred the
death to have occurred in hospital'.
        I wrote the above paragraph 14 years ago (Rees, 1969) when
I was a family physician with hospital privileges in Mid-Wales.
The hospital was a small, friendly unit where the patients were
well known to the nursing staff. Despite this I invariably
noted a change in the status of patients once they entered hospital, and my personal relationships with them, such that I
never could attain the level of intimacy and communication I
had before admission.
        The distress of dying at home is different from that of
dying in hospital. Compared with those who die in hospital
(Rees, 1972) people dying at home are more likely to be fully
alert shortly before death; less likely to be suffering from
vomiting, incontinence or bed sores; and less likely to have
unrelieved physical distress. Dying at home may have certain
medical advantages over death in hospital, besides the social
and psychological advantages of home deaths. But not everyone
can die at home. There are those who need institutional care,
particularly in our society where one third of elderly people
live alone. Fortunately special facilities are being created

158

for these to have in-patient terminal care, notably in hospices and continuing care units.

An additional factor is that bereavement itself has the characteristics of a disease with an intrinsic morbidity (Parkes, 1964; Birtchnell, 1975) and mortality (Rees and Lutkins, 1967; Parkes et al., 1969); while improved support during bereavement can reduce morbidity (Parkes, 1980).

TERMINAL CARE

Death can be accurately located in time, whereas dying is of variable and uncertain duration. It contains the episodes of mental and emotional distress classified by Kübler-Ross (1970) and the elements of physical and emotional distress recorded by Exton-Smith (1961), Hinton (1963), Rees (1972), Cartwright et al (1973) and Doyle (1980). Weakness is the commonest complaint of the terminally ill patient and is usually associated with pain, anxiety, depression, awareness of dying, disfigurement, unpleasant body odours, respiratory distress, nausea or visual disturbance, and aggravated by financial problems and spiritual uncertainties. Unrelieved pain is common in terminal illness and effective pain control can and should be achieved. The table given below, taken from the report by Rees (1972) refers to the prevalence of symptoms 24 hours before death.

Table 14.1: Prevalence of symptoms 24 hours before death

Physical Distress		Level of Consciousness	
Vomiting	28%	Comatose	40%
Bedsores	30%	Stuporose	20%
Faecal incontinence	30%	Confused	12%
Urinary incontinence	46%	Fully alert	28%
Indwelling catheter	26%		
None of these	26%		

An important function of those engaged in terminal care is to provide support to the family before and after bereavement in an endeavour to reduce the morbidity associated with bereavement. In this respect terminal care is now an aspect of preventive medicine.

It was with these basic concepts in mind that I accepted the full time post of Medical Director of St. Mary's Hospice in May 1981.

HISTORICAL BACKGROUND

The idea of a hospice as a place of rest for the incurably ill was conceived by Sister Mary Aikenhead of the Irish Sisters of Charity, in the late nineteenth century. The first modern hospice was established by Dame Ciceley Saunders in 1967, when she opened St. Christopher's Hospice in Sydenham, South London, at a capital cost of £250,000 which was raised from local and charitable sources. Similar units were rapidly established throughout the country. The first to open in the West Midlands was St. Mary's Hospice.

The National Society for Cancer Relief also financed special in-patient facilities for cancer patients. In 1979, the Society decided to extend their work to the establishment of nursing teams specialising in the domiciliary care of terminal cancer patients, and allotted £2½ million to this purpose. It was from these concepts of Dame Ciceley Saunders and the National Society for Cancer Relief, that St. Mary's Hospice and its Home Care team were developed.

St. MARY'S HOSPICE

The decision to establish St. Mary's Hospice was taken in 1973. The first patients were admitted in March 1979 and the hospice was officially opened by Princess Alexandra on 10 June 1979.

The capital cost of establishing the 25-bedded hospice was approximately £450,000 of which £415,000 had been raised from charitable and private sources by March 1979. It is an independent charity separate from the National Health Service. However, 29 per cent of its running costs are paid by the NHS. This payment is for in-patients only and not for the Home Care Team. The National Society for Cancer Relief contributed £35,000 to pay salaries of the Home Care Nursing Sisters and 25 per cent of that of the Medical Director for three years only.

THE HOME CARE TEAM

The Home Care Team consists of three full-time nursing sisters; a part-time (two-thirds) social worker; a part-time doctor; and a part-time voluntary clerk. The hospice allotted office space, provided the administrative and financial infrastructure and made available hospice beds to which patients could be admitted by the Home Care Team.

The aims of the team are:

1. To provide the specialist care required by the terminally ill and support for their families during the illness and bereavement.
2. To raise the quality of life of each patient to the highest possible level.
3. To assist in the training of medical students, nurses and clergy (of all denominations) in the specialist care of those who are dying.

Domiciliary Care of the Terminally Ill

In the year ending March 1982, when the team had only two
nursing sisters, 2066 domiciliary visits were made, comprising 214 first visits, 1797 re-visits and 55 bereavement visits
to the relatives of people who died at home. The patients
who were re-visited included 27 patients discharged from the
hospice.

In the same year 261 patients were admitted to St. Mary's
Hospice, and there were 237 deaths. Most patients had terminal cancer, but a few chronically sick non-cancer patients
were admitted for periods not exceeding two weeks, so that
relatives might have respite from nursing duties. The Home
Care Team does not look after those because its funding comes
from a cancer relief organisation.

Inception

When St. Mary's Hospice opened the staff had a great deal to
learn about the care of dying patients. A similar problem
arose when the Home Care Team was established. The idea of
nurses and social workers specialising in the domiciliary
care of the terminally ill was new, and the team had much to
learn. They were fortunate in being able to draw on previous
experience in hospital and community. The first nursing
sister to be appointed to the Home Care Team spent four weeks
working on the wards at St. Mary's Hospice and six weeks with
the Home Care Service attached to St. Joseph's Hospice, South
London, before establishing the first domiciliary care service for terminal cancer patients in the West Midlands. The
first social worker to be appointed to the team established
in-patient services, liaison with statutory and voluntary
bodies, a considerable commitment to the home care patients,
development of the bereavement counselling service and the
teaching of social work students seconded to St. Mary's
Hospice. The staff developed close working relationships
with district nurses, community physicians, social workers
and hospital doctors in the area. That this was achieved
without controversy was due to their understanding of the
area, the tact with which they presented their case and the
need for the service. They were helped by the hospice policy
of welcoming visitors, the widespread desire of people that
terminal care should be done well and the high regard already
given to the work done at St. Mary's Hospice. This was achieved without the problem of acceptance encountered by Home Care
Teams in some other areas.

Operation of the Home Care Team

Referrals to the Home Care Team are accepted from general
practitioners and hospital doctors only. Use of a standard
application form ensures that the team receives basic social
and medical data and relevant hospital letters. Requests are
dealt with quickly, usually within 48 hours. When the referral is from a hospital doctor the general practitioner is

contacted by telephone and his approval sought. This consent
has been withheld twice only, because of special family problems. The general practitioner has a key role in domiciliary
care and is ultimately responsible for prescribing the treatment advised by his specialist colleagues.

The Home Care Team meets daily. The discussion tends to
be informal and is often lighthearted. This is a necessary
balance for the serious work undertaken by the team and the
stressful situation so often encountered. The senior nursing
sister organises the work of the team and, in consultation
with her colleagues, allocates the daily visits. The team
meets formally every Friday morning under the chairmanship
of the senior nursing sister for a full discussion of each
patient under its care.

Four visits to newly referred patients are usually made by
the doctor accompanied by a nursing sister, a pattern similar
to that used in Edinburgh (Doyle, 1980). This allows the nursing sister to discuss problems with the family, whilst the doctor is conferring with the patient. The visit usually ends
with the doctor and nurse discussing the situation with the
patient and family. Re-assessment visits are usually made by
a nursing sister or a social worker alone, except when they are
accompanied by students.

Patients are referred to the Home Care Team for the following reasons:

1. As a preliminary step to obtaining hospice admission.
2. To assist with symptom control, especially pain
    relief.
3. To provide general support for the patient and
    family.
4. At the request of a nurse, social worker, relative
    or patient.

The Home Care Team recognises the primary responsibility of
general practitioners and community nurses towards their patients, despite the fact that the support given by Primary
Care Teams to dying patients is highly variable, as is pointed
out by the Working Group on Terminal Care (1980), which states
that 'unfortunately some GPs are not fully aware of what can
be achieved in domiciliary care and it seems likely that the
most distress as well as the least occurs at home.'

The nursing sisters with rare exceptions visit all home
care patients. Thirty-four per cent of patients are seen by
the social worker and 66 per cent are visited by the terminal
care physician who unfortunately has time to see only a proportion of referred patients. The home care nurses work closely
with the terminal care physician, discussing with him changes
in family situations and symptoms. Through them the physician
monitors symptom control, advising the family and general
practitioners on drug changes. With experience the nursing

sisters acquire their own confidence and expertise in this field. Robottom (1981) has questioned the need for specialist nurses in domiciliary terminal care, arguing that this is a function of the district nurse. But such arguments see confrontation where none exists. There is a place for both skills and only 50 per cent of our patients are attended by a district nurse when we first visit. Our home care nurses are prepared to help with nursing care but not to supplant the district nurse. All our patients are given the Home Care Team's telephone number, with the assurance that they will not be considered a nuisance if they seek help at unsocial hours. District nurses do not provide this type of service. In the crisis of a terminal illness familiar faces seem particularly important and for this reason the home care nurse often seems to be contacted in preference to the general practitioner. In order to cope with these night calls, and to ensure that their availability is not abused, the nurses have on-call rota for the nights and week-ends. The home care nurses do not provide a night sitter service themselves, but arrange either for night sitters from the Social Services Department, or for private night nurses paid for by Cancer Relief.

Social Worker. The social worker is employed for 30 hours each week and spends 2/3 of this time with the domiciliary care service. She sees 34 per cent of home care patients who are referred to her by the senior nursing sister. She ensures that families receive the full benefits available from statutory and charitable sources, including grants for extra nourishment, fuel and heating, telephones, clothing and bedding, taxi fares, convalescent holidays and contributions to the cost of night nursing.

Social workers find their role at St. Mary's Hospice particularly rewarding. The work provides a wide range of contacts which have a warmth and friendliness lacking in other areas of social work. The social worker has an important counselling role in the field of bereavement. The first assessment of the need of bereavement help is made by the social worker in consultation with other staff members immediately after a death. Nineteen point five per cent of next-of-kin were visited. The problems dealt with included loneliness, depression and financial troubles. Four weeks after bereavement all next-of-kin receive a letter asking if they need further help. Seventy seven point five per cent replied and asked for help, while non-respondents were telephoned at home and in this way effective contact was made with 89 per cent of next-of-kin. The importance of this type of support in endeavouring to reduce the morbidity associated with bereavement is considerable.

Domiciliary Care of the Terminally Ill

EVALUATION

Other factors being equal, it makes economic sense to treat people at home. The cost of domiciliary care, including the care
of the terminally ill, is small compared to the cost of in-
patient care. This is appreciated by the West Midlands Regional Health Authority which relates a measurable cost benefit to
the NHS with maintaining a home care service for the terminally
ill (Regional Strategy 1979-1988). It is reflected also in the
annual budget of St. Mary's Hospice where the cost of maintaining the Home Care Team is very small compared with the cost of
the in-patient service.

It is difficult to evaluate the team's effectiveness objectively, especially in the present early stage. There are
however some pointers. Requests for the help of the Home Care
Team are increasing rapidly. In 1983 the 60 patients supported
at home by the team are more than double the number cared for
twelve months ago and a vast increase on two years ago. Two
point three per cent of patients cared for by the team are doctors or their wives. The high referral rate may reflect esteem
for our domiciliary care service, or the tensions or problems
(Maddison, 1974), associated with caring for a seriously ill
medical colleague or his wife. There is not a similar high referral rate of medical patients for our in-patient service. Another finding is that 3.7 per cent of home care patients are
overseas immigrants, mostly of Asian origin, compared with 1.7
per cent of patients admitted at St. Mary's Hospice. This suggests that our Home Care Team meets the requirements of terminally ill Asian patients. In general, immigrant patients referred to the Home Care Team tend to have larger families who
live nearby and to be slightly younger than those referred for
hospice admission. This supports the findings of Cartwright et
al (1973), that there is a relationship between age, family
size and place of death. The immigrants referred to the Home
Care Team all seem to have large families and to be relatively
young.

Until 1981, the likelihood of a patient referred to the
Home Care Team dying at home was no greater than the national
average. But in 1982, the pattern changed and 45 per cent of
Home Care Team patients actually died at home. This is shown
in Table 14.2 below. This can have important implications for
the survival of close relatives because there is evidence
(Rees and Lutkins, 1967) that mortality following bereavement
increases significantly if the primary death occurs in the
hospital.

Table 14.2: Place of death

	Percentage of deaths in		
	Hospital	Hospice	Home
England and Wales	59	7	33
Home Care Team (1981)	12	54	34
Home Care Team (1982)	11	44	45

This can have important implications for the survival of close
relatives. We know that there is an increased risk of coro-
nary thrombosis following bereavement (Parkes et al, 1969);
that those most likely to die soon after bereavement are young
widowers (Kraus and Lilienfeld, 1959; Rees and Lutkins, 1967),
and that when a person dies in hospital the subsequent mortality amongst surviving relatives is twice that occurring amongst
relatives of people dying at home (Rees and Lutkins, 1967).
This variation in mortality amongst surviving relatives means
that dying at home is safer for next-of-kin than dying in hospital, a further argument in support of domiciliary care for
the dying.
      The following reports illustrate the work of the Home Care
Team:

Case 1
This lady lived 30 miles away and was visited by the physician
only. The patient knew that she had incurable rectal cancer
and she wished to die at home. Pain and vomiting had been
troublesome but had been well controlled with four-hourly
intramuscular injections of stemetil and diamorphine, until the
district nurse experienced difficulty in locating adequate
sites for further injections. Attempts to replace the injections with oral medication resulted in recurrence of the symptoms. The problem was easily solved by administering diamorphine only subcutaneously continuously using a syringe driver.
The patient remained comfortable at home until she died four
weeks later.

Case 2
This patient was referred by the general practitioner at the
wife's request. She wished to nurse him at home but refused
help from the district nurse. The patient had metastatic
brain disease with intellectual impairment and intermittent
headaches. Pain control was achieved with regular oral anal-
gesics. During the following six weeks, the home care nurse
visited the home 14 times to monitor symptom control, and to
support the family. She was able to persuade the wife to
accept help from the district nurse. The patient died peace-
fully at home one Sunday morning. The wife was unable to contact the general practitioner. She phoned the home care nurse

who visited immediately, confirmed death, straightened the
body, contacted the general practitioner and funeral director
and remained with the wife for four hours until family members
arrived.

Case 3

This very deaf man, with lung cancer, was referred by the
general practitioner at the daughter's request. Although he
was bed-ridden and incontinent of urine and faeces he was well
cared for by the daughter and the district nurse. When asked
why she wanted our help, the daughter replied, 'I need someone to talk to; someone to tell me that what I am doing is all
right'. The home care nurse visited seven times and established a close bond with the family. When the patient died
three weeks later, she was invited to the funeral.

The following letters are selected from the many received
which illustrate the appreciation by relatives of the work of
the Home Care Team:

Letter 1

'My dear colleague - I must formally notify you of the death
of S.L. on Sunday, 1 May, at home. I would like to take this
opportunity of thanking you personally and your community
nursing service for the superb care and attention that he has
received these last three months. It has been most appreciated
by himself, his family and I. Many thanks, Yours, Family Dr'.

Letter 2

'Although it is now six weeks since N. died, it really seems
like yesterday to me, and I am writing to thank you, Joan and
Pat and all the staff for the wonderful help you gave N. and
me and all the family. It was largely due to your continuing
care that N. and I felt able to deepen the quality of our life
together, and I had not realised what that could mean to us
both. The constant encouragement and understanding of the
Home Care Team made N's last days seem a real achievement, and
I know it helped him to keep his gallant courage to the end.
His children have told me that living through his death with
Joan's loving concern and help made it easier to accept and I
have found it a healing experience in spite of my grief. With
grateful thanks, Yours, J.B.'.

THE FUTURE

Local expansion of domiciliary care services for terminal cancer patients is proceeding rapidly. In 1979 the West Midlands
contained no nurse or doctor with the specific task of helping
terminal cancer patients at home. In 1983 12 home care nurses
were employed for this purpose in the Region and two doctors
had specific responsibilities for the terminal care of patients
at home. Four of the 12 nurses are based at St. Mary's Hospice,

two are at a Continuing Care Unit and two are attached to each of three new hospices. Three other new domiciliary care teams are planned, one without an in-patient base and two based on hospitals. Home Care Teams work best from established bases like hospices but they can survive without these facilities. In one district specialist nurses are provided by the Health Authority with office facilities only, which is reasonable as an interim measure but not as permanent policy. In another area a specialist nurse is employed by a hospice to work from a Health Centre in an experiment to improve co-operation with the Primary Care Team.

In the past payment for domiciliary care services has come mainly from private or charitable sources, especially the National Society for Cancer Relief. This pattern is likely to change. The NHS can be expected to provide an increasing contribution towards the finances of domiciliary terminal care. In neither system is payment required from the patient. At present, private patient insurance schemes do not accept responsibility for hospice or domiciliary terminal care. But changes are likely and eventually some payment will be allowed by private insurance towards domiciliary terminal care.

The optimum size for a domiciliary care team is difficult to assess. Each team needs a doctor, a social worker, clerical help and probably six nurses. Larger teams become difficult to handle. Domiciliary terminal care services are likely to extend their role to caring for patients other than those suffering from cancer. Some involvement with cardio-pulmonary and cerebro-vascular diseases seems inevitable. Already home care teams are helping with the care of neurological diseases especially motor-neurone disease. Expansion of domiciliary care in these fields may be based on hospitals or hospices. The co-ordinating units may be departments of radiotherapy, geriatrics, hospital-based departments of general practice, or, as at present, independent hospices.

Interest in hospice-based units for the domiciliary care of terminally ill children has enlarged since the opening in 1982 of the world's first hospice for the care of terminally ill children, Helen House in Oxford. Discussions are taking place on the possibility of establishing such a hospice in this region, while there is considerable pressure on St. Mary's Hospice to establish a separate children's unit.

CONCLUSION

The work of St. Mary's Hospice and of its Home Care Team has led to much new thinking in how dying patients are cared for. It is to be hoped that through formal and informal education improvements will continue both in terminal care of the dying and in many cognate areas of care.

REFERENCES

Birtchnell, J. (1975) 'Psychiatric breakdown following recent bereavement', British Journal of Medical Psychology, 48, 379–90

Cartwright, A., Hockey, L. and Anderson, J. (1973) Life before death, Routledge and Kegan Paul, London

Doyle, D. (1980) 'Domiciliary terminal care', The Practitioner, pp. 575–82

Exton-Smith, A. N. (1961) 'Terminal illness in the aged', Lancet, 1, 305–8

Hinton, J. M. (1963) 'The physical and mental distress of the dying', Quarterly Journal of Medicine, 32, 1–21

Kraus, A. and Lilienfeld, A. (1959) 'Some epidemiologic aspects of the high mortality rate in the young widowed group', Journal of Chronic Diseases, 10, 207–17

Kübler-Ross, E. (1970) On Death and Dying, Tavistock, London

Maddison, D. (1974) 'Stress on the doctor and his family', Medical Journal of Australia, 2, 315–8

Parkes, C. M. (1964) 'Effects of bereavement on physical and mental health – a study of the medical records of widows' British Medical Journal, 2, 274–9

Parkes, C. M. (1980) 'Bereavement counselling: does it work?', British Medical Journal, 281, 3–6

Parkes, C. M., Benjamin, B. and Fitzgerald, R. (1969) 'Broken Heart: a statistical study of increased mortality among widowers', British Medical Journal, I, 740–3

Rees, W. D. (1969) 'Bereavement', in Austin H. Kutscher (ed.) Death and Bereavement, Charles C. Thomas, Illinois

Rees, W. D. (1972) 'The distress of dying', British Medical Journal, 3, 105–7

Rees, W. D. and Lutkins, S. (1967) 'Mortality of bereavement', British Medical Journal, 4, 13–16

Report of the Working Group on Terminal Care (1980) Standing Sub-Committee on Cancer of the Standing Medical Advisory Committee

Robottom, B. 'The role of the specialist nurse in terminal care, MacMillan Seminar on Communication, Abingdon, pp.19–20. A MacMillan Report, National Society for Cancer Relief

West Midlands Regional Health Authority: Regional Strategy (1979–1988), pp.169–73

Chapter Fifteen

EDUCATION IN CARE OF THE ELDERLY

Bernard Isaacs

INTRODUCTION

When the Department of Geriatric Medicine of the University of
Birmingham was set up in 1975 it instituted programmes of education for medical undergraduates and postgraduates; and for
other professional and non-professional groups. Early on advice was received from the Professor of Education who said,
'Never write down a syllabus, or within two years it will require an Act of Parliament to change it'. There has been a
lot of experimentation. The department has drawn on the experience of practitioners in all fields to assist in teaching and
has used as additional teachers the patients themselves and
their carers, many of whom have proved highly articulate, generous, and insightful in their comments. Some of the continuing courses will be described.

UNDERGRADUATE MEDICAL EDUCATION

The Birmingham medical student, like his counterpart in other
medical schools, is expected to amass much information. In his
fourth year, after studying anatomy, physiology, biochemistry,
pharmacology, pathology and the clinical sciences he is exposed
for rather less than two weeks to his main course in geriatric
medicine. Until then his concept of 'a geriatric patient' may
well have been an elderly person with severe multiple disabilities awaiting transfer from an 'acute' ward to a 'long-stay'
ward. Modern geriatric medicine is as yet a closed book to
him. But we resist filling him, in our two weeks, with facts
about the physiology, pathology and pharmacology of normal and
abnormal ageing. We assume, rightly or wrongly, that medical
students are 'turned-off' by geriatric medicine. They have
lived for a year in the world of 'acute medicine' and 'acute
surgery'. There they will indeed have seen many old people;
but the emphasis is on single diseases in younger people which
can be unequivocally diagnosed and firmly treated. Geriatric
medicine cannot compete for their attention in that way, so it

must be taught differently.

We try to get across those aspects of geriatric medicine which are not practised by doctors and not conducted in hospital. Geriatrics depends on the work of many people, including the patient himself, the relatives, nurses, physiotherapists, occupational therapists, social workers, speech therapists, neighbours, home helps, voluntary organisations and a host of others. Hospital is a temporary place of refuge for the management of complex problems which is needed only until the patient is able to return home. The traditional activities of the physician, such as ward rounds and out-patient clinics, play their part but are not distinctive; and students spend little time as spectators of the consultant. Instead they go out to the patient's home, in company with those who care at home; or to the special locations where specific treatments are provided. Thus students visit with home helps, community nurses, domiciliary physiotherapists, geriatric health visitors and general practitioners; and go to day hospitals, day centres, residential homes, sheltered housing projects, a terminal care hospice, the limb-fitting centre, the centre for the visually handicapped, a stroke club or any other facility towards which their curiosity guides them. Wherever they go they talk to patients and relatives, try to find out what it means to be old and disabled, and learn how the services are comprehended and appreciated by their recipients.

Organisation

The structure of the medical course in the fourth year and the resources to be found in a large city makes this system possible. During 16 consecutive fortnights between September and April, 16 groups of ten students each, rotate through the two-week teaching period in geriatric medicine. There are ten consultant physicians in geriatric medicine in four hospitals, so one student is attached to each consultant firm for his two-week period. Consultants provide the student with both a 'table d'hote' and an 'a la carte' menu; i.e. obligatory activities which assume a minimum knowledge of the service; and optional activities chosen from a list which allows students to develop special interests. The students are conscientious and attendance approaches close to 100 per cent.

Time is made available in the second week, (and these, by the way, are shortened three-and-a-half day weeks) for students to prepare a project which they have to present verbally on the final morning and briefly, in writing, within four weeks. The project is on any topic of their choice related to old age, but is based on their own experience during the course, and preferably contains quantitative information which they have collected themselves. Library projects are not wanted. Despite the extremely short period available and the other demands on their time the students have set and maintained a high standard of projects. The choice of topics is remarkably wide, ranging from straightforward descriptions of patients and services, with critical comments; through little surveys of patients' hearing, vision, dentures, feet, clothing, meals, medication, sleep and the like; and on to larger issues about old people in society, both in factual matters like their income, heating, home safety and social networks, and in attitudinal matters like their views on death and euthanasia. Each student presents his paper to the group of ten and to a few of the teachers, and each presentation is followed by a discussion to which the other students contribute their experience. It all makes a very educative morning.

The course appears to be acceptable to the students as judged by such remarks as 'We did not know there was so much to it'; 'We had never met a health visitor (or home help, community nurse or occupational therapist) before', and best of all, 'It's all out there'.

The course has evolved from earlier versions (Fleetwood-Walker, Mayer and Isaacs, 1983). The time to evaluate the course will be once the students have become doctors and are working in busy medical and surgical wards. Will they acquire the host culture, or will they retain something of the insights which they gained when they were studying geriatric medicine?

The Grandparent Survey

Birmingham students have a two-year pre-clinical course,and their entry to clinical medicine is preceded by an introductory lecture course. The department of geriatric medicine is allotted one morning in this course, and we are asked to provide the students with background information about the demographic, epidemiological and social aspects of health and illness in old age.

In order to try and make this interesting and meaningful we arrange for them what we call the 'Grandparent Survey'. One week before the meeting of the class each student is issued with a form on which he provides information about his four grandparents. For those who have died we ask the year of birth, the year of death and the cause of death if known. For those who are still alive we want to know year of birth, current living arrangements, perceived state of physical and mental health, and possession of motor car and telephone. The forms take students only two or three minutes to complete, and the department staff analyse them and produce tables for presentation to the students.

The students are asked to identify biases in the sample. The first response is usually that it is social class biased, which we accept; but the students are then asked to indicate if they have a parent who is a doctor (there may be about 20 of these) and a grandparent who was a doctor (there is seldom more than one of these). This indicates the social mobility of the two generations. The second bias which they detect is usually that the age distribution of the grandparents differs from that of the elderly population as a whole because of its starting point from people of a uniform age. It takes them longer to appreciate that the sample differs from 'all old people' in the absence of the unmarried and the childless, who form a significant component of applicants for institutional and community services. The grandparents are a favoured group and the findings of the survey might be expected to reflect a better situation than that in the population as a whole.

The data on age at death is defective. Students have no opportunity of consulting their parents before filling in the form, and their knowledge of the year of death and of birth of their grandparents, is incomplete. Causes of death usually reflect family lore, and terms like 'old age', 'senile decay' and 'something fatal' take their place beside the more sophisticated medical diagnoses. Sufficient material usually emerges to demonstrate that heart disease, cancer and stroke comprise two-thirds of all deaths in the sample; and that the First World War has stamped its impress on the cohort. The differing life expectancy of males and females is very clearly brought out. Statistics from national samples are presented and the students are given an opportunity of comparing these with their sample results, and of learning about the variability of national census and survey data.

The age and sex distribution of living grandparents shows the expected two- or three-to-one preponderance of females with a peak age around 80. Living arrangements show a predominance of grandfathers and grandmothers living together up till about 75; widowed grandmothers living alone after that; and a few, extremely old, grandparents living with a family member other than the student's parents. Three-generation families, of which students are members, are rare. The figures also demonstrate the large number of grandparents who have no living family members within 20 miles. While most grandparents live in a household with both telephone and motor car it is those who live most distant from their families who are least likely to possess these amenities. Almost the entire sample lives at home, with only about 5 per cent in hospital, residential home or private nursing home.

The medical questions relate to the presence of limitation of mobility, falls, incontinence, intellectual impairment, visual and auditory handicap. Visual and hearing defects are by far the commonest disturbances. About 10 per cent of the sample turn out to have dementia. Falls are experienced by many grandparents, incontinence by few. All these findings are contrary to the students' expectations; but all are supported by survey data which is presented alongside the grandparent material.

The final question is whether on the whole the grandparents are thought to be content with life. Every year the great majority of students record their grandparents as being 'content on the whole', although they recognise that they are likely to see their grandparents at their brightest.

The Brains Trust

In the second half of the introductory morning students present written questions about old age for discussion by a panel of 'experts'. The panel includes one or two people beyond the age of 75. We have had a general practitioner, a retired Vice-Chancellor, an ex-Lord Mayor, a volunteer organiser. We also have a senior house officer in geriatric medicine, and either a social worker, an officer in charge of a residential home for the elderly, a home help organiser, or someone else with a day to day knowledge of old people. A resident of an old persons' home is always recruited.

The questions follow familiar patterns from one year to another. Euthanasia appears in one guise or another. Many questions imply criticism of residential homes or geriatric wards or unrest at the way in which old people are required to live. Other questioners propose a better deal for old people in a variety of ways, not always realistic. After the panel members have responded to the questions, usually with a sharp dash of realism, students join in the discussion. The level of interest is lively; but the star is usually the oldest member of the panel. Students register surprise that someone over the age of 80 or 90 can actually present a coherent and witty argument, and probably this is the best piece of education they get. The questions allow the painless imparting of facts as well as the exchange of opinions; and the students applaud spontaneously at the end of the session.

An evaluation of the degree to which the survey material is retained by the students is planned, using as a control group students to whom the same facts are presented in a more conventional way. We want to test whether material which has been generated by the class is more memorable than that produced from an outside source. We wonder whether surprise is a factor in making facts memorable. We are interested, for example, in learning whether students who, before the survey, believe that about half of the elderly population were in hospital or institutions, would be likely to remember the true figure of 5 per cent because they had generated this from their own sample. Or did they believe their own grandparents to be so different from other old people that they rejected their findings and retained their earlier misconceptions? As yet the study has not been completed. The least that can be said is that the students' attention is held during the lecture session.

SENIOR REGISTRAR TRAINING PROGRAMME

There are ten senior registrar posts in geriatric medicine in the West Midlands Region. The doctors holding these posts have been qualified for five or six years and are undergoing a four-

year training to become consultant physicians in geriatric
medicine. Their training is largely through gaining practical
experience in the hospital units where they work. There is a
rotational scheme to vary their experience and they have the
opportunity, if they so desire, of spending one or two of
their four years in departments of general medicine, the better
to equip themselves for a post of consultant physician with an
interest in geriatric medicine, in which general medical duties
are combined with those in geriatric medicine. They take part
in the administrative work of their units, undertake research,
and gain special experience in psychogeriatrics. For one
half-day once a fortnight they take part in the Regional Training Programme.

The objective of the Regional Training Programme is to
make sure that the senior registrars know all that will be required of them when they become consultant physicians in a department of geriatric medicine. This mainly means the range of
skills which are subsumed under the name 'administration'.I see
this as meaning familiarisation with every job of every person
with whom they will come into professional contact. They therefore spend a series of afternoons learning about the training,
skills, and experience of physiotherapists, occupational therapists, speech therapists, social workers, hospital and community
nurses and health visitors. We also include in our study afternoons chiropodists, dental practitioners, ophthalmologists,
home help supervisors, meals on wheels organisers, ambulance
drivers, trade unionists and other health and social workers and
voluntary organisations. The senior registrars also visit
community resources which are potentially useful to our clients.
These include residential homes for the elderly, day hospitals,
day centres, the limb-fitting service, terminal care hospice,
and many others; while further sessions are devoted to the administration of the NHS; the organisation of Regional and
District Health Authorities, the health care planning teams,
the work of the District administrator and so on.

The most popular and valuable part of our studies are
visits to other departments of geriatric medicine. We have
one of these visits each month, and the senior registrar, if
there is one, in the host unit plays a major part in organising the visit. At each visit the host team describe the catchment area of the service, the distribution of its beds, the
history and development of the service, its philosophy and
mode of functioning, its interfaces with general medicine,
psychiatry, social services, general practitioners; the mode
of operation of its services, and any special innovations
which it has introduced. This may be supplemented by a clinical or research presentation of some special activity of the
unit.

There is also deliberate training in becoming a consultant.
The mechanism whereby consultant vacancies become available is
explained by the Regional personnel officer. Job descriptions

for fictitious posts are circulated and volunteer applicants
from amongst the senior registrars are subjected to mock interviews. Two meetings a year are devoted to presentations by
senior registrars of their own research work. Some sessions
deal with research methodology and statistical analysis. The
course enables the senior registrars to get to know one another
well; and gives the professor a guide to their qualities and
to the progress of their training.

THE ELDERLY BY THEMSELVES

Once a year we run a study day in which the lectures are given
by patients and their relatives and the audience consists of
the professionals - doctors, nurses, therapists, social workers, care assistants and home helps. We contact ex-hospital
patients, attenders at the day hospital, home help clients,
residents in local authority homes, disabled people, notably
the blind, and relatives of the recently deceased. They come
and talk generously but honestly about their experiences in
contact with our services. They are told not to hesitate to
criticise when criticism is justified, and they do so frankly
and fairly. The articulate elderly speak on behalf of the in-
articulate elderly. They praise our intentions and sometimes
our achievements and point gently but shrewdly to our short-
comings. This is a great learning experience for us and a
great teaching experience for them. The usual comment is 'Why
don't we do this more often?'.

THE GREAT INCONTINENCE ROADSHOW

The use of a flippant title is deliberate. It encourages
schools of nursing throughout the Region to hold study days on
incontinence to which we bring a group of experts who raise
the local level of interest. These study days are always very
well attended by nurses from hospital and community, by residential care staff and home helps and their supervisors. Physiotherapists, occupational therapists, and social workers come
along too; and we have even had some general practitioners and
hospital doctors. The roadshow has a standard shape. After a
short introduction the audience breaks up into groups to discuss questions prepared in advance. These include:

1. When do you use catheters?
2. Do you find charting helpful?
3. Do you have regular toiletting rounds?
4. Do you use pads on the bed?

The small groups are non-threatening to nurses and there is no
'report-back'. The groups are intended to break the ice, to
mix hospital and community staff, and to teach the fact that
there may be more ways than one of approaching a mundane task,

and better reasons for doing something than 'It has always been done that way'. This may sound a condescending set of objectives, but the change which we are trying to stimulate is more likely to be effected through emulation of a peer than from the words of an expert. Moreover, after the group work, the audience seems to be more receptive to the speakers. These include a urologist who talks about the causes of incontinence and investigation of the patient; a nurse who speaks about incontinence management in hospital; and a second nurse who speaks of the management in the community. We then have a demonstration of equipment and its use. In the afternoon we hear from a manufacturer about the problems of providing a product which meets patients' requirements. This is followed by a talk by the local supplies officer, who explains the way in which new equipment can be obtained in a district, and the difficulties which this might entail. At a final session the ideas of the day are drawn together and ways of implementing the lessons learned are stressed. There is always good follow-up locally after the roadshow. Often study groups are formed which continue the discussion and which undertake efforts to implement new processes and methods of care suggested by the study day.

THE 20-80 GROUP

Twenty per cent of the population aged 80 and over suffer from dementia, a fact which gives the title to this group. It is a loose association of people with special knowledge of the elderly patient with mental impairment. The group includes geriatricians, psychogeriatricians, community psychiatric nurses, the staff of residential homes for the elderly mentally infirm and of day centres for the same group. Members of the group are willing to be called upon to take part in educational activities in which their skills can be of assistance.

We have circulated District Medical Officers and Directors of Social Service in the West Midlands Region to indicate our willingness to take part in discussions on the development of services for the elderly mentally infirm. We have been invited to run seminars and study groups, and to sit round the table with planning groups. The latter has been particularly successful, because groups thinking of setting up new services have been enabled to test their ideas against the practical exprience of members of the 20-80 group who have been through the difficulties and identified the obstacles.

WORK IN RESIDENTIAL HOMES

The department welcomed an invitation from a residential home for the elderly to undertake education inside the home. The officer in charge had concluded that when only one or two members of staff went off to a course, whatever they learned was

not implemented on their return. She thought that better results might be obtained from bringing the education to the
home. She had arranged for all her staff to be on duty every
Monday, so that on one day each week there were sufficient
people on duty to enable the job to be done properly, including participation in education.

After initial shyness even the untrained staff began to
contribute their observations. The discussion proceeded by
tentative exchange of ideas and explanations. The staff selected incontinence, stroke illness and dementia as the topics on
which they sought enlightenment. We learned much from the
staff about the problems they experienced, and how they interpreted and responded to residents' behaviour. Sometimes we
were able to offer our own interpretations. This worked extremely well as an educational experiment for both sides, but
it would be difficult to take on a continuing commitment to
the homes within the catchment area of a district geriatric
service. On the other hand not all homes ask for such help,
and a monthly visit to one or two homes could be sustained
without too much strain on the department.

INNOVATIONS IN THE CARE OF THE ELDERLY

It is no coincidence that these meetings bear the same title
as this book. They were set up jointly by the University Department of Geriatric Medicine and the Regional Office of the
Department of Health and Social Security Social Work Service
in an effort to disseminate throughout the Region good innovative practices that were operating successfully in one part of
the Region.

Each meeting identifies a project which is well established and researched and invites the providers of that project to act as hosts and main speakers of the meeting. The
project can be in health, social services or housing and the
audience consists of senior members of staff of local authority Departments and District Health Authorities. The hosts
present information on the innovation, how it was established,
how it is administered, what it costs. Its operation is described by staff working day to day in the service; and the results of any formal evaluation are presented. If it is convenient for the facility to be visited this is part of the programme. During the rest of the study day comparable innovations in other parts of the Region are described, and there is
much time for discussion of the relative merits of different
approaches to a common problem. The success of a session is
judged in the short-term by the number of contacts made, and
the number of people who ask for additional information about
the innovation.

Education in Care of the Elderly

CONCLUSION

We have tried to teach our students and colleagues that many
old people are not ill; that not all who are ill are in hospital; and that most care is not given by doctors. To learn
even that is to make a small but significant beginning in an
improved understanding of the needs of old people and their
carers.

POSTSCRIPT

Education in geriatric medicine is provided in virtually all
United Kingdom medical schools. In the 13 schools with academic departments of geriatric medicine which have professorial heads, there tends to be a better organised course and a
greater allocation of curriculum time than in those schools
where responsibility for teaching rests with the local National Health Service consultants. In this case teaching may be
confined to a brief unstructured clinical experience, based on
occasional visits to geriatric wards or residential homes for
old people; although in some cases an excellent course is
provided.
In medical schools with academic departments the clinical
course in geriatric medicine usually takes place in the fourth
year of the curriculum, that is, the second clinical year, and
lasts from one to four weeks. Teaching is mostly by small
group methods, and includes bedside clinical teaching, case
presentations, case conferences,seminars, discussion groups,
visits to places of interests, and meetings with other professionals. Domiciliary visits are included as logistic constraints permit. One medical school has a combined course in
geriatric medicine for students of medicine and nursing. Another combines the teaching of the physical diseases of old
age with those of the mental diseases. The medical students
are widely reported as responding very positively to the
course, and commenting favourably on the enthusiasm of the
teachers. Community experience is particularly welcomed.
Participation of the department of geriatric medicine in
other areas of the medical school curriculum is varied but limited. Very few students study academic gerontology as part
of their course in human growth and development, which in most
departments seem to stop at puberty. A number of departments however contribute to the teaching of other branches of
clinical medicine, and to courses in social medicine and psychiatry.
The content of teaching varies with the philosophy of departments. The range of attitudes might be illustrated by the
time devoted to teaching of incontinence of urine. Some departments take the view that this is a common and distressing
symptom in old age which is poorly taught elsewhere in the
curriculum, and that the department of geriatric medicine must

accept a major responsibility for ensuring that students are well equipped by them to understand and deal with this problem. At the opposite extreme are the departments which take the view that geriatric medicine has to disassociate itself from the image that it is all about incontinence, so the teaching should concentrate on the exciting work which this new specialty is tackling and the excellent results it is achieving in other aspects of diagnosis and rehabilitation. The emerging student's view of geriatric medicine will no doubt be coloured by which of these opposing schools of thought he encounters in the course of his medical education.

REFERENCE

Fleetwood-Walker, P., Mayer, P. P. and Isaacs, B. (1983) 'A New Approach to Course Development in Geriatric Medicine', Medical Education,17, 95-9

Chapter Sixteen

THE SOCIETAL CONTEXT OF INNOVATION IN CARE OF THE ELDERLY

Helen Evers

INTRODUCTION

Today's provisions for care of elderly people have evolved in
a piecemeal fashion. This has resulted from initiatives arising at all levels, from the state to the individual, in response to changing definitions of sociopolitical and demographic imperatives. The process has a long history, and the
early 1980s feature continuing preoccupation with the implications of our ageing population and how best to respond in
a period of economic austerity. The innovators of the 1980s
and beyond may well require extraordinary resourcefulness if
the quest for service development and improvement through
innovation is to continue. Detailed accounts of the experiences of innovators of the middle and late 1970s will make an
important contribution.
     In this chapter, I will raise some general points about
the political and institutional context in which innovative
services emerge and subsequently impact on clients, on existing and on other innovative services. These are:

1. Policy framework of innovation
2. New services: expectations and realities
3. Effects on consumer choice
4. Broadened professional roles and the consumer
5. New services and changing levels of demand
6. Division of labour among new, evolving and established services
7. Substantive contribution to policy and practice
   debates

1. POLICY FRAMEWORK OF INNOVATION

The process of innovation appears in various guises at different levels of government. Central government responds to social, demographic and political pressures; and influences
the climate in which top management at a more local level is

setting its priorities and operating policies. Through legislation and fiscal measures, goals and constraints are identified in a general way. Central policy documents set out government views in a more explicit fashion, and indicate the kinds of responses which are expected at other levels. 'Priorities for Health and Personal Social Services in England' (DHSS, 1976) is an important example, which helped set the scene for many of the innovations described in this book. So far as services for the elderly were concerned, the main emphasis was on so-called community care as top priority, with more efficient use of hospital and residential resources and greater attention to maintaining or restoring the capacity of elderly people to live independent lives at home. As part of this endeavour, 'Priorities' called for new co-ordinating machinery among the various services at all levels: health, social services, housing and voluntary organisations. Working groups came into being within the health service, at regional level and below, also within the social services and across service boundaries.

At this middle management level locally, individual innovators often emerge, and certainly did so in the aftermath of 'Priorities'. Such people have a far more concrete view of the practical issues with which central government policy pronouncements are concerned, and are in a strong position to identify and respond to gaps in services at the practice level. Being organisationally close to practice, these middle-level service providers are also in a position to take account of the needs and problems of elderly people as seen by the elderly themselves, and by those who care about and for them. The state service innovations described in this book were initiated variously by semi-autonomous medical practitioners (Pike, Chapter Four; Harrison, Chapter Ten; Gaspar, Chapter Eleven and Rees, Chapter Fourteen); by middle- or senior-level managers within a particular local service area (Daffern, Chapter Five; Priestnall, Chapter Six; Frazer, Chapter Seven; and Hamilton, Chapter Nine) or through collaboration across service boundaries at middle- or senior-level (Keegan, Chapter Twelve and Pettitt, Chapter Thirteen). Innovations also come from organised voluntary effort: Staunton, Chapter Eight, provides an example.

The innovative spirit in and around Birmingham, England is strong and the 1970s have seen the development of diverse but unco-ordinated new services. Since all those described in this book have been developed in the same geographical area, they have become part of the same social and service infrastructure relating to a given elderly population. Gathering accounts of innovative services and their development in this way offers an unusual and timely opportunity to consider the intended and unanticipated consequences of a change in one part of the system for the modus operandi of other parts.

2. NEW SERVICES: EXPECTATIONS AND REALITIES

Although an innovator's proximity to service provision - as
direct service provider or manager - may enable him to see and
respond to gaps in services, it may also pose problems for him
in predicting how the expectations of the new service will be
fulfilled in practice. Once the idea for an innovative service
is launched, staff or volunteers are employed and clients recruited, the service often takes on a life of its own. The
innovator whose idea has come to fruition must usually relin-
quish or share ownership and control of his ideas and mission.
The way the service develops will be affected by its partici-
pants - service providers and recipients - and the wider social,
service and economic context in which it operates. Unforeseen
problems, benefits or opportunities may arise, particularly
where interconnections with other services are concerned. At
Highbury Day Centre, for example, some of the operational policies defined at the planning stage became modified in practice
when specific staff appointments had been made and links established with other professionals concered with Highbury's
clients (Keegan, Chapter Twelve).

3. EFFECTS ON CONSUMER CHOICE

The bulk of health and social care of elderly people is not
done by services at all, but by families, particularly the
women of the family, and other lay carers. The views of elderly people and their lay carers are not always taken into
account when decisions about service provision are made
(Fairhurst, 1977) and patterns of service allocation often
fail to match patterns of need as felt by elderly people and
their carers (Equal Opportunities Commission, 1982; Nissel
and Bonnerjea, 1982).
    Innovative services for elderly people create opportuni-
ties to discover and respond to a wider range of people's
needs. As a result, elderly people and their lay carers may
have some freedom of choice if and when they seek help from
formal or voluntary services. For example, the various types
of support which can be provided by the Home Help Service
(Daffern, Chapter Five) should allow the old person's pre-
ferences and normal lifestyle to be taken into account when
considering an appropriate pattern of service provision. The
Volunteer Stroke Scheme (Staunton, Chapter Eight) adds a fresh
alternative or adjunct to state and other voluntary services
for stroke victims. When the variety of services on offer increases, it becomes particularly important that relevant information about availability of and eligibility for services is
easily obtainable, so that potential clients do not end up
feeling bewildered by the different services on offer.
    Increased freedom of informed choice for elderly people
is valuable not least because dependency among the elderly is

often socially created or reinforced: exclusion from the labour market through retirement dramatically reduces income, and elderly people are among the poorest members of society (Walker, 1981; Townsend, 1981 and Phillipson, 1982). The structure of our social institutions does little to challenge the view of elderly people as second class citizens, and there are few immediate prospects of major change in this regard. But the creation of a wider range of innovative services makes a positive contribution to protecting the autonomy of elderly people. For example, features of a more effective hospital geriatric service (Harrison, Chapter Ten) - planned short stay, acceptance of emergency admissions - may increase people's chances of resuming, or continuing to live relatively independent and satisfying lives.

4. BROADENED PROFESSIONAL ROLES AND THE CONSUMER

Another consequence of introducing new services is that professional workers may adopt far broader roles than would be conventionally the case. For example, domiciliary physiotherapists may become involved in tackling patients' social or environmental problems (Frazer, Chapter Seven). They might seldom encounter such problems when working with patients in hospital. Nurses in a home care team for terminally ill patients likewise confront all manner of patients' and their families' concerns over and above the illness itself (Rees, Chapter Fourteen). While this broadening of professional roles may have obvious benefits for clients, it is as well to be alert to the potential difficulties. Freedom of choice may actually become limited through the client's involvement with a service provider who has become a 'Jill of all trades'. Another possibility is that unproductive and confusing overlaps in function may be the result when more than one such provider becomes involved with an old person.

5. NEW SERVICES AND CHANGING LEVELS OF DEMAND

In providing a service where none existed before, or in modifying a service so as to improve 'quality of life' for the elderly population at large, pressures on other services may be lessened in some respects but increased in others. Innovative modification of high-rise housing stock, for example, can improve the standard of housing for elderly people (Priestnall, Chapter Six). Providing appropriate housing probably makes a direct contribution to enabling elderly people to remain in their own homes in the longer term. This in turn has implications for future demands on community support services, institutional facilities, family and lay carers.
    Screening clinics (Pike, Chapter Four) may affect not just the quality of life of a GP's elderly patients who are living at home, through diagnosing and ameliorating previously

unreported conditions; but also demands for other services.
If patients' expectations about their state of health and quality of life are changed through regular visits to the screening clinic and any subsequent medical treatment, different
levels of demand for services may ensue. Anticipatory care
may well allow people to remain living at home for longer, but
in the end this may increase demand for institutional services
through prolonged active life. Voluntary workers may help
elderly people, for example stroke victims and their families
to obtain from service organisations information, aids and
support which had previously been lacking; thus increasing
demands for formal help. Staunton (Chapter Eight) remarks
that very often, volunteers are more used to asking questions
and getting answers than are their clients. Thus they may
enable clients to articulate their unmet needs to service providers.

6. DIVISION OF LABOUR AMONG NEW, EVOLVING AND ESTABLISHED
    SERVICES

Creating a new service causes upheaval in inter-service expectations and responsibilities. I will explore this in relation
to services for the elderly mentally infirm. In common with
much of the rest of Britain, and further afield as well, the
record of the West Midlands in providing for the needs of this
group is not particularly outstanding. The advent of a new
day centre could be interpreted by some GPs as a facility to
take on the bulk of responsibility for care of elderly mentally
infirm patients. But where the number of places provided is
fewer than the number of places needed, an obvious policy
choice is to provide a minimal level of service, for example
one day a week, to the greatest possible number of sufferers.
This can only work in practice where the GP sees his role as
continuing to provide the major support (Keegan, Chapter
Twelve).
     To carry out comprehensive assessment of people referred
for specialist residential care, on offer from a social
services department, one obvious strategy is to seek collaboration with psychiatrists and geriatricians, as described by
Pettit (Chapter Thirteen). But where a psychiatric service
for demented people and their relatives is in its early stages
of development (Gaspar, Chapter Elven), collaboration with
psychiatrists may be difficult to secure in practice.
     If a specialist home for elderly mentally infirm people
is both to avoid the extremes of institutionalisation and to
continue offering a resource to the wider community, then some
population turnover following the assessment procedure is essential. Pettitt analyses the problems associated with maintaining some turnover of residents. As only a tiny minority of
those people referred are likely to be able to return home,
then places must be sought in other institutions: local

authority residential homes, private sector homes or continuing-care hospital beds. Very often other residential homes face more demand than they can meet from other sources and unless staff grades and numbers are on a par with the specialist facility, severely mentally infirm clients are unlikely to be wholeheartedly welcome. In the private sector, the elderly mentally infirm are perhaps the hardest to place. Increasingly, geriatricians are working towards a greater emphasis on active approaches to treatment and rehabilitation of patients with a view to discharging them from hospital (Harrison, Chapter Ten). Thus they too are unlikely to volunteer the use of their beds to house long-stay mentally infirm patients. Where a psychogeriatric service is, all to commonly, lacking or rudimentary, the problem is compounded. The Department of Health guidelines (eg Ministry of Health, 1965; DHSS, 1972) as to which authorities and institutions should have the responsibility to provide long-term institutional care appear highly specific, and are in practice controversial. Thus longstanding debates about the appropriate division of labour are bound to re-surface when an innovative service - a specialist home for elderly mentally infirm people - enters the arena. It is to be hoped that eventually these kinds of issues, rendered more visible through the advent of innovation, will achieve sufficient impetus to trigger authoritative review of service and professional boundaries where they act as impediments to integrated service planning and practical provision, to the likely detriment of clients.

7. SUBSTANTIVE CONTRIBUTION TO POLICY AND PRACTICE DEBATES

Examples of controversial topics among providers of services for the elderly are appropriate directions for housing policy; whether screening clinics should be more widely established and, if so, what their focus should be; the policy and practice of integration or segregation of mentally infirm old people in residential care; and future patterns of development for hospital geriatric medicine. Detailed accounts of the origins, processes and outcome of innovative services by practitioners make an essential addition to professional and research-based literature on these issues. Practical information on the way that specific pioneering schemes operate, and the benefits and problems that arise, should contribute to policy deliberations at all levels about which are the most promising kinds of developments to encourage on a wider scale.

CONCLUSION

The innovations described in this book represent unco-ordinated responses at or near practice level, to gaps or inadequacies perceived in existing services. Recognising gaps and succeeding in doing something about them depends on a coincidence of many factors, including an 'innovative spirit' working in a climate which is supportive or in which opposition can be brooked. Climate is a product of public opinion, government policy, legislation and the translation of these into practice through the many layers of government and service organisation. Processes of innovation and of interrelationships among services can be clearly seen by gathering accounts of particular service developments within the same locale and climate, as has been done in this book.

Comprehensive catalogues giving outline descriptions of new services for old people can be found elsewhere: Ferlie (1983) for example has collected summaries of British innovations in community care of elderly people from the sponsors of the services, including social services departments, health authorities, housing departments and voluntary organisations. A sourcebook of that kind is of great value in indicating the range of initiatives. The preceding chapters of this book complement Ferlie's approach, by uncovering the backgrounds of particular schemes and their relationships with other services.

Very often descriptions of service provision, whether of established or new services, are couched in idealistic terms. Seldom does one find open discussion of difficulties to be overcome and the failure, as well as success of different strategies for tackling them. The accounts of new services in this book provide an opportunity to take a fresh perspective. The importance of attention to processes and problems of initiating services - which is possible through focussing on a limited number of innovations - strongly influenced the decision to limit comprehensiveness of this book's coverage to a single geographical area. As governments and climates change, fresh service initiatives will emerge, and in the interests of policy and practice development in the 1980s and beyond, documenting the experiences of innovators of the 1970s and early 1980s is of more than passing value.

REFERENCES

Department of Health and Social Security (1972) 'Services for mental illness related to old age', NHS Memorandum HM(72)71, Cardiff
Department of Health and Social Security (1976) Priorities for Health and Personal Social Services in England, HMSO, London
Equal Opportunities Commission (1982) Caring for the elderly and handicapped, EOC, Manchester
Fairhurst, E. (1977) 'Teamwork as panacea. Some underlying assumptions'. Unpublished paper read at Annual Conference of the Medical Sociology Group of the British Sociological Association, University of Warwick
Ferlie, E. (1983) Sourcebook of initiatives in the community care of the elderly, Personal Social Services Research

Unit, University of Kent, Canterbury

Ministry of Health (1965) 'Care of the elderly in hospitals and residential homes', NHS Memorandum HM(65)77, London

Nissel, M. and Bonnerjea, L. (1982) Family care of the handicapped elderly: who pays? Policy Studies Institute, London

Phillipson, C. (1982) Capitalism and the construction of old age, Macmillan, London

Townsend, P. (1981) 'The structured dependency of the elderly: A creation of social policy in the twentieth century', Ageing and Society, 1: 5–28

Walker, A. (1980) 'The social creation of poverty and dependency in old age', Journal of Social Policy, 9: 49–75

Sylvia Daffern, formerly Principal Officer, Home Help and Night
    Watch Service, City of Birmingham Social Services Depart-
    ment
Helen Evers, Senior Research Fellow, Department of Sociology,
    University of Warwick, Coventry
Fred Frazer, District Physiotherapist, South Birmingham Health
    Authority
D. Gaspar, Consultant Psychogeriatrician, Hollymoor Hospital,
    Northfield, Birmingham
R. Griffiths, District Medical Officer, Central Birmingham
    Health Authority
Barbara Hamilton, Continence Advisor, South Birmingham Health
    Authority
J. F. Harrison, Consultant Physician in Geriatric Medicine,
    Selly Oak Hospital, Birmingham
Bernard Isaacs, Charles Hayward Professor of Geriatric
    Medicine, University of Birmingham
Mary Keegan, formerly Manager, Highbury Day Centre
R. Liddiard, Director, City of Birmingham Social Services
    Department
Dorothy Pettitt, Inspector, Services to the Elderly, City
    of Birmingham Social Services Department
L. A. Pike, General Practitioner, Birchfield Health Centre,
    Birmingham
David J. Priestnall, Senior Assistant City Housing Officer,
    City of Birmingham Housing Department
Dewi Rees, Medical Director, St. Mary's Hospice, Selly Oak,
    Birmingham
Eileen Staunton, Supervisor, Volunteer Stroke Scheme, South
    Birmingham Health Authority

DATE DUE

APR 0 4 1985		
MAY 2 5 1990		
MAY 0 7 1990		